**GENERAL REFERENCE**

# RAISING THE SUCCESSFUL CHILD

How to encourage your child on the
road to emotional and learning competence

**Sylvia Clare**

**How To Books**

Cartoons by Mike Flanagan

**British Library Cataloguing in Publication Data**
A catalogue record for this book is available from the British Library.

© Copyright 1998 by Sylvia Clare.

First published by How To Books Ltd, 3 Newtec Place,
Magdalen Road, Oxford OX4 1RE. United Kingdom.
Tel: (01865) 793806. Fax: (01865) 248780.
email: info@howtobooks.co.uk
www: http://www.howtobooks.co.uk

All rights reserved. No part of this work may be reproduced or stored in an information retrieval system (other than for purposes of review) without the express permission of the Publisher in writing.

*Note:* The material contained in this book is set out in good faith for general guidance and no liability can be accepted for loss or expense incurred as a result of relying in particular circumstances on statements made in the book. The laws and regulations are complex and liable to change, and readers should check the current position with the relevant authorities before making personal arrangements.

Produced for How To Books by Deer Park Productions.
Typeset by PDQ Typesetting, Stoke-on-Trent, Staffs.
Printed and bound by Cromwell Press, Trowbridge, Wiltshire.

# RAISING THE SUCCESSFUL CHILD

### Some other titles in this Series

Achieving Personal Well-Being
Becoming a Father
Building Self-Esteem
Controlling Anxiety
Having a Baby
Helping Your Child to Read
Learning to Counsel
Managing Yourself

Parenting Pre-school Children
Self-Counselling
Successful Grandparenting
Successful Single Parenting
Survive Divorce
Surviving Your Partner
Thriving on Stress
Unlocking Your Potential

*Other titles in preparation*

The How To Series now contains more than 200 titles in the following categories:

Business & Management
Computer Basics
General Reference
Jobs & Careers
Living & Working Abroad

Personal Finance
Self-Development
Small Business
Student Handbooks
Successful Writing

Please send for a free copy of the latest catalogue for full details (see back cover for address).

# Contents

| | | |
|---|---|---|
| List of illustrations | | 7 |
| Preface | | 9 |
| **1** | **Understanding emotional competence** | 11 |
| | Recognising emotions | 11 |
| | Communicating successfully | 15 |
| | Case study | 18 |
| | Clarifying communication outcomes | 19 |
| | Case studies | 19 |
| | Defining success | 22 |
| | Exploring the importance of emotional competence | 23 |
| | Learning together | 25 |
| | Summary | 27 |
| **2** | **Parenting skills and styles – teacher or hypocrite** | 28 |
| | Evolving parenting skills | 28 |
| | Learning lessons | 30 |
| | Exploring the power in parenting | 32 |
| | Learning by example | 33 |
| | Recognising hidden agendas in parenting | 35 |
| | Case study | 36 |
| | Summary | 38 |
| **3** | **Prioritising for parents** | 39 |
| | Assessing priorities | 39 |
| | Prioritising children | 40 |
| | Balancing needs | 41 |
| | Case study | 41 |
| | Summary | 45 |
| **4** | **Avoiding the over-protection trap** | 46 |
| | Making mistakes is essential | 46 |
| | Learning lessons in six dimensions | 47 |
| | Case study | 48 |

|   |   |   |
|---|---|---|
|   | Protecting or inhibiting | 49 |
|   | Case study | 50 |
|   | Putting off the lessons | 51 |
|   | Case study | 54 |
|   | Welcoming the lessons | 55 |
|   | Case study | 55 |
|   | Summary | 56 |
| **5** | **Disciplining or devastating your child** | **57** |
|   | Understanding discipline | 57 |
|   | Blocking learning | 58 |
|   | Avoiding shame and guilt | 60 |
|   | Controlling or caring | 61 |
|   | Learning styles for parents | 62 |
|   | Summary | 68 |
| **6** | **Understanding love** | **69** |
|   | Defining love | 69 |
|   | Letting go and allowing your child to learn | 70 |
|   | Supporting your child to confront fear | 71 |
|   | Letting go of fear for parents | 73 |
|   | Trusting your child | 75 |
|   | Summary | 75 |
| **7** | **Using stories as metaphors** | **76** |
|   | Developing imagination | 76 |
|   | Using empathy | 78 |
|   | Accessing the unconscious mind | 79 |
|   | Teaching throughout history | 81 |
|   | **The stories** | **83** |
|   | The little holly tree | 85 |
|   | Thinking about the story | 89 |
|   | The fox and the blue grapes | 97 |
|   | Thinking about the story | 101 |
|   | The legend of wildwood | 106 |
|   | Thinking about the story | 117 |
| Glossary |   | 122 |
| Further reading |   | 124 |
| Useful addresses |   | 125 |
| Index |   | 126 |

# List of Illustrations

| | | |
|---|---|---|
| 1 | Basic structures of the brain | 12 |
| 2 | Evolution of mums | 29 |
| 3 | The hierarchy of needs | 42 |
| 4 | Directions of learning | 47 |

# Preface

This book is written with full acknowledgement for all the learning opportunities I have had in my years of teaching and working with young people. They taught me so much, but above all showed me that inside even the most difficult child or teenager there is a loving and gentle person wanting to be free. They are only waiting for an opportunity to express themselves as they truly are. Yet society, which is all of us, labels them as difficult and traps them in unhappiness and limits them from revealing who they really are and what they are capable of achieving.

In private practice I have worked with mature adults who were still waiting for their inner child of joy and spontaneity to be released. They are the ones who have had the courage to face their fear and leave it behind. They have learned the true meaning of peace and have learned to love their inner child.

This book is based on the learning experiences I have shared with all, in an attempt to make the future easier and gentler for everyone. It is aimed at everyone and anyone who works with children, as a parent or in any other capacity, and who wants to change society and create a more accepting and loving environment for all.

Special thanks go to Matthew and Ben for being my loving, forgiving and very patient teachers as I learned how to be a good parent, and to Cordelia, Morag and Caying for the time we shared together. They all helped me to be a better person.

*Sylvia Clare*

# 1
# Understanding Emotional Competence

**RECOGNISING EMOTIONS**

We are accustomed to a rich vocabulary which describes the range and nuance of our emotional responses to different experiences. We assume the words represent emotions which are different from each other. By analysing the rudiments of each emotion, we find that experientially there are only two emotions, **fear** and **joy**. Everything else originates here.

The importance of the emotion is decided by the intensity of physical response. The perception of the cause or source of the emotion tells us it is fear or joy, or any variation of these.

Both fear and joy originate in a part of the brain called the **limbic system**, which has the ability to identify a source, e.g. a threat, and respond milliseconds before conscious awareness of the danger.

The limbic system has two capacities, **memory** and **learning**. The predominant experience in childhood is the predominant emotional experience in adulthood because the limbic system has learned to respond in the biased way according to experience. So our brain can be programmed to experience joy or fear as a dominant response, according to the kind of childhood we have had. As parents we can decide how to programme our child, and as adults we can recognise and modify our own programming.

## Experiencing fear

Fear is an essential warning response to an unexpected situation. It is an appropriate emotion in life-threatening situations such as walking near a precipice or facing an out-of-control car. In these situations the **amygdala** (part of the limbic system) is programmed to kick in with an automatic response commonly called fight or flight (see Glossary). In both the above cases flight would be the most appropriate response and we would recognise that through our perceptual interpretation of the events and environment around us.

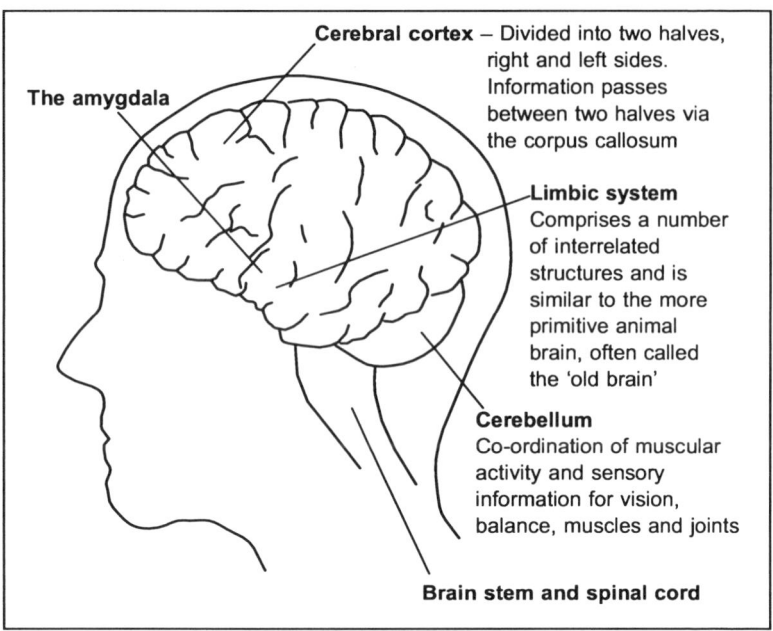

Fig. 1. Basic structures of the brain.

Previous learning tells us how to differentiate between the responses in each situation, the former requiring a careful retreat from the edge and the latter requiring fast movement away from the vehicle's path. A young child will often freeze in a situation because they have not learned what else to do and this is the safest option in most cases.

To feel fear is not to be cowardly. To show fear is a sensible and honest response, part of self preservation, but to be ruled by fear is to be emotionally unable to function for your own best interests.

*Fear or excitement?*
If presented with a challenge we might find our heart thumping, throat feeling dry, stomach churning and hands sweating, as in any of the above situations. Whether we interpret that as fear would depend entirely on our perception. For instance, when facing an exam – something important and unknown – most students will feel all of the above physiological responses. What will differ will be their interpretation of these feelings as either fear or excitement. The former will likely result in a retreat and the latter will engender a 'go for it' approach. Which student will succeed? Well, both might but

# Understanding Emotional Competence

any guess would suggest student B will do better and will certainly be more likely to want to repeat the experience, feeling that exams are a good challenge to rise to. Student A will probably avoid anything more than is absolutely essential to 'get out of school free' and never sit another exam in their life.

The initial fear response kicks in whenever we face change, i.e. the unexpected.

*Variations on fear*
- Anger – fear of life not going as you had intended for yourself, of losing control.
- Frustration – fear of not getting what you want or perceive yourself to need.
- Anxiety – fear of failure, loss of face, fear of the future.
- Sadness – fear turned against ourselves, fear of loss or change.
- Guilt – fear of being wrong, of being accused of something or hurting someone.
- Shame – fear of getting 'found out', of being less than expected or demanded.
- Regret – fear of losing something worth keeping.
- Vengefulness – fear of being 'a loser', of coming second, of not having the upper hand.
- Bitterness – fear of being cheated, of having less than you think you deserve.
- Jealousy – fear of having less than someone else.
- Hatred or dislike – fear of that in another which reflects that behaviour/attitude in yourself.
- Possessiveness – fear of losing that which you have, fear of betrayal of others.
- Self pity – fear of taking responsibility for your own actions and experiences.
- Loneliness – fear of being unloved/unwanted, fear of being alone with self.

## Experiencing joy
This is essentially the opposite to fear and is energising and

uplifting. If we experience a predominance of the following emotions, we are likely to be contented and successful:

- Enthusiasm – joy of opportunities being presented.
- Elation – joy of the experience in the present.
- Calmness – joy of general sense of well-being, spiritual contentment and health.
- Peacefulness – joy of sense of intimacy and fulfilment, joy of being alone with self.
- Competence – joy of developing skills and using them.
- Confidence – joy of exploring and being yourself.
- Self esteem – joy of knowing yourself and being true to that self.
- Achievement – joy of positive outcomes following sustained effort.

These are simplified explanations and need discussion for specific situations. The essential thing is recognising which emotion you are experiencing and its origins.

**Exercise 1.1**
To begin with, choose a time when you are not in full flow of a strong emotional force but, maybe, feel a bit out of sorts, niggled or about to face a challenge.

- Think about which parts of your body are reacting to this emotion. Is it stomach, neck, back, head etc?
- What purpose do these feelings have, what are they telling you about life's experiences?
- What does this experience tell you about yourself?
- What constructive action would you take to end the difficulty?
- Is there anyone you need to talk to in order to resolve this?
- What do you need to say or do to resolve the situation and achieve the outcome that is for the best possible good for yourself and others?
- Does your desire conflict with the best possible good for yourself or others?

- What else could you choose to think and feel?
- Do you need/want to feel this emotion any longer?

Hopefully this exercise left you feeling more objective and more conscious of your emotions. Ironically most people forget to repeat this exercise with positive feelings. It is easy to take them for granted and overlook the ingredients. By exploring good feelings, we can re-create them using this recognition and understanding, thereby allowing us more choice in how we feel day to day.

## COMMUNICATING SUCCESSFULLY

Parents have the power of gods over young children. The use and understanding of this power is essential to parenting the successful child and is based on how and what we communicate to them.

Communication occurs on two levels. The first is the choice of **actual words**. This is a small part of the understanding, about 20 per cent. The second and bigger part of the communication is called the **meta-message** and is to do with all the assumptions, expectations, body language and contextual aspects of the communication.

The rest is made up from the following:

- basis of interaction, intended outcome
- balance of power/authority
- emotional impact
- facial expressions and eye contact
- body posture and clothing worn
- environmental influences (context, venue, formal or informal)
- previous experiences with this person
- previous experiences in similar situations with others
- assumptions about intentions of other
- own intentions for interaction.

Intuitively we learn to read all of these cues to reach the final understanding of a message and although the choice of words is important, the rest is often where the difficulties lie.

## Communicating empathy

As a parent it is important to know how our children feel so that we can respond to them sensitively and validate their experiences, taking them into account.

- We cannot relate to their feelings if we do not know our own.
- We cannot expect them to express their feelings to us if we do not teach them by example how to do this.

Can you think back to a time when, as a child, you wanted to express yourself and no one took you seriously?

- How did this leave you feeling?
- Were you keen to communicate with this person again?
- Were you keen to communicate with anyone again?

## Developing empathy

Empathy is the ability to imagine the situation from the other side, to put yourself into someone else's shoes and to form relationships based on mutual appreciation and understanding. Empathy is the skill of recognising that other people have a right to their point of view and taking this into account when you interact with them. As parents it is essential to take into account your child's point of view for two reasons:

1. Your child then perceives that their experiences are considered significant and worthy of consideration, therefore the child feels valued and worthy of consideration.

2. Your child recognises your skill in empathising with them and learns the same skill by following your example.

A good exercise for refining empathy skills is to think back to a difficult situation you experienced with someone else. Closing your eyes makes this more effective. Keep it in the present.

## Exercise 1.2

Briefly run through the incident in your mind, everything you feel, think, say and do.

# Understanding Emotional Competence

- What do you intend by those behaviours?
- How are they interpreted by the other party?
- What areas or aspects result in a difficulty?
- Is there a lack of two-way communication about what you really feel?
- Have you actually said what you really felt and wanted to say?
- Have you said things that only gave clues to what you wanted to say? What were they?
- Are you saying the opposite of what you wanted to say?
- Is the outcome as you had hoped for or intended?

There are no right or wrong answers. Your answers reflect your present position and should give you food for thought. The more you work with exercises like these, the better your understanding and self knowledge will become.

Now imagine yourself in your partner's position, trying to listen to you. Make sure that you are in *their* position and not as you would like them to be, or as you think they should be.

- How easy is it for them to understand what you are saying?
- What level of frustration do you experience in being understood by your partner (ie you)?
- What do they actually say in response to you?
- What is your understanding of their intended outcome?

The second stage of this exercise is to imagine yourself in your partner's position and run through all the above questions from their position. This requires concentration because you will have to imagine being your partner trying to imagine what it feels like to be you watching them. Follow me?

This is full empathy. Perhaps they felt equally frustrated in their attempts to get their point of view listened to. Perhaps they also failed to say exactly what they meant for fear of losing face or being criticised for their experiences.

If you have difficulty being understood in relationships with parents, children, partners etc it is a reflection of how well you communicate and how easily they can understand you. You should also consider how effectively you listen and take account of their position. Most rows would begin and end as calm discussion if all communications worked.

**CASE STUDY**

**Keith and Jane are unable to communicate**
Keith and Jane are both divorcees who have set up home together. They each have one child. Jane lived alone for some time before meeting Keith and is not worried about being single again but would prefer to stay in the relationship. Keith walked straight out of his marriage and an affair, and latched onto Jane. His biggest fear is to be alone. They have been together for three years and are finding it increasingly hard to agree on anything, even small decisions about the house. Jane suggests counselling. Keith says he would rather end the relationship than go to see a counsellor. Jane concedes. The relationship is easier for a while.

Two years later they are still arguing and Jane says she's had enough. She again suggests counselling or she feels that it is over for her. Keith agrees initially but then repeats that he would rather end the relationship than go for counselling. Jane agrees the relationship is over. Keith becomes very angry over the next weeks and begins to bully Jane, shouting a lot and telling her that the relationship is over. She is not arguing with him. Then he starts throwing things round in the house and tells her that they can live together for another five years, until the children have grown up. Jane asks him to leave. He shouts even more loudly that their problem is that he just can't communicate with her any more, he is clearly very distressed. Jane does not feel able to communicate with Keith any more.

- What is happening between Jane and Keith and their communications?
- Does Jane say what she means?
- Does Keith say what he means?
- Why can't Keith communicate with Jane?
- Why can't Jane communicate with Keith?

Is Keith saying what he thinks will get Jane to back down again? Is his anger a sign of his fear of being alone and frustration that his attempt to manipulate Jane is not working this time? Fear fills the relationship for Keith and he operates from this perception. Jane allowed herself to be bullied and manipulated before, which set up an expectation in Keith that this was how to keep the relationship together. His attempt to say what he really means comes through with such inner conflict that he expresses it aggressively. Jane cannot hear what he has said because of the anger in his voice and the meta-message he is giving. He wants submission from Jane and is fearful and shaken when it does not happen as he intends.

## CLARIFYING COMMUNICATION OUTCOMES

Whenever we are talking about something it is important to understand where the discussion is left. Think back to your worked example above. Was the outcome of this discussion:

(a) a complete resolution and reconciliation?
(b) a compromise and avoidance of further dispute?
(c) another issue which remains unresolved and damaging?

If you can answer yes to (a) then you are well on the way to successful communication skills. If you answered yes to (b) then you are possibly never dealing with anything and leave an undercurrent of difficulty which can build into resentment. If you answered yes to (c) then it would be a good idea to practise the above exercise as often as possible in all your interactions and notice the benefits to yourself and your life.

All relationship crises are failures in communication and lack of empathy. This is true in professional, academic, personal and social relationships. Success is based on the ability to use these skills positively.

### Abusing empathy skills
Some people have excellent empathy skills but use them to manipulate others. Utilising these skills in a negative way achieves a measure of success, which acts as a reinforcement to continue the behaviour. The success will always be short lived and cause more problems in the long run.

## CASE STUDIES

### Keith wants to feel secure
Keith has difficulty saying what he feels. His father was rarely

approachable and, as a child, Keith was scared of him. No matter how hard Keith tried to please his father, he felt a failure because he did not win approval but was encouraged to continue working for it. It was a 'no win' situation for Keith.

As an adult Keith frequently changes job and tries to work alone. He often misses opportunities for promotion and developing his potential, yet achieved overall Grade As at school. He has never maintained a steady relationship. He has regular affairs alongside any longer relationships, including a marriage and becoming a father. Although he is desperate to settle down and feel secure, he flirts with anyone who responds because he has learned how to charm and win superficial approval.

For Keith love is a battle of wills, of seeking and gaining approval, of fighting for control and dominance. He cannot respond to requests or suggestions from his partner because he hears it only as yet another rejection of all the effort he is making. He 'tests' his partners to see how much they love him, and tries to force Jane into loving him unconditionally, no matter how badly he treats her. He threatens to end the relationship in order to make Jane 'try harder' for him but feels fear when she begins to withdraw from him. Keith is left feeling hurt and confused at why all the women in his life treat him like this. He just needs to find 'the right partner' and keeps on looking, flirting and desperately seeking approval from wherever he can.

- Which dominant emotion is Keith feeling?
- What is the long term future likely to be for Keith?
- What is the basis for Keith's emotional and relationship failures?

The fear of failure and rejection kicks in for Keith as soon as he starts to become close to someone and blocks all real communication. He uses his understanding of feeling hurt as a basis for attacking his partners with the intention of undermining their confidence and sense of security. By making them feel or appear less confident and relaxed, he feels more confident by contrast. This is a perceptual difference. Keith feels fear and assumes the source of his fear is his partner, ie external. He does not realise that it is a fear programme in him and has little to do with his partner. He reacts to his fear and the loving partner becomes undifferentiated from the hostile attacker, so he counterattacks. He uses empathy to hurt and to wield power, as his father did over him.

Childhood is the learning ground for this approach. There is a

# Understanding Emotional Competence

particular style of communication which leads to these difficulties, call **the double bind**. First introduced as a theory by Bateson in the 1950s, it has become a basis for much work in the areas of family therapy. It denotes a system where the communication purports to be about one thing but there is a deeper and more significant, unspoken message occurring at the same time. No one actually says exactly what they mean but they give clues and attempt to manipulate other members of the family into doing, thinking or saying what they want. Then they can deny responsibility for the outcome because they didn't actually say it. Parents use it with their children in many ways. It puts the recipient in a 'no win' situation, where their own feelings are totally discounted and they have to find a way to demonstrate their love for the parent in order to keep their approval.

### Keith manipulates Megan's feelings

Megan and her father Keith have been living with Jane and her son Sam for five years now. Megan is close friends with both Jane and Sam. When Keith and Jane separate after many rows, Megan wants to stay friends. Jane says she would like that too but that Megan must tell Keith. Her father then highlights the perceived injustices that Jane and Sam have apparently heaped on him and ridicules them. The next time Megan sees them, she is hostile and tells Jane she doesn't want to see her and Sam any more. Jane says she understands and if Megan changes her mind she will be happy to see her.

- What are the choices which Megan has been given in this situation?
- How has empathy been used?
- Why is this an example of the double bind?
- Was it really Megan's choice?
- Who listened to Megan's wishes?
- Whose needs were considered before hers?
- What is the meta-message to Megan?
- What emotions has Megan experienced with this episode of her life?
- What is the basis behind Keith's behaviour?

At a guess she had experienced most of the following: separation and loss of friendship, guilt, being wrong, frustration, regret, sadness and fear of similar rejection from her father. Her father can point out that it is Megan's choice because he hasn't actually said 'don't see Jane and Sam'. Megan has been made to feel sorry for him instead, and to prioritise his feelings in order to prove her love for him. Keith feels too insecure to allow Megan to continue as friends with Jane and Sam *because if she still likes them they cannot be as bad as all that*, can they? So he loses his justification for rejecting them. He cannot accept that he has another failed relationship.

Keith's behaviour may finally bring rewards and an appearance of success in achieving his intended outcomes, but is this success and is it what he wanted?

## DEFINING SUCCESS

Success comes in many shapes and forms. One of the most important rules is to avoid imposing your own set of values for measuring success onto your child. If you let them devise their own, then they will work for it and stick to it with a motivation that would inspire you. A goal imposed from an external source, even from a beloved parent, is only achieved to please the parent, and therefore has limited intrinsic value to the child other than to receive praise. The more the child is freed from the pressure of external referencing for their own life, the better they will succeed in their life. The intrinsically governed individual does not get drawn by other people or become easily persuaded against their better nature.

We will be referring to this theme several times during the book and in many different contexts. One of the first researchers into success was Abraham Maslow. He was a humanistic psychologist who looked at levels of achievement in the lives of many successful people like Einstein, Eleanor Roosevelt, Walt Whitman, Spinoza, Abraham Lincoln, Thomas Jefferson. (Yes, only one female, but this research was carried out in the 1950s and 1960s.) He called success '**self actualisation**'. The important point is that he also recognised that there is no such thing as the perfect human being (1970).

### Characteristics of self actualisers

(a) they perceive reality efficiently and accept uncertainty

(b) non-judgemental of self and others

(c) spontaneity of thoughts and behaviours

# Understanding Emotional Competence

(d) problem centred instead of self centred
(e) unusual sense of humour
(f) able to look at life objectively
(g) highly creative and original in approaches to life
(h) retaining an independence but not purposely unconventional
(i) concern for the welfare of all living beings
(j) deeply appreciative of basic life experiences
(k) establish deep satisfying relationships with a few people
(l) peak experiences
(m) enjoy privacy and solitude
(n) embrace attitudes of equality to all
(o) hold strong moral or ethical standards to which they adhere.

## Behaviours leading to self actualisation

1. Experiencing life with enthusiasm, absorption and concentration.
2. Experimenting with new things and welcoming challenges instead of taking the safe path.
3. Listening to your own feelings in evaluating experiences instead of accepting the conditions of tradition, authority or of the majority.
4. Avoiding double bind, game playing behaviours and being honest.
5. Being prepared to be unpopular when your perceptions do not coincide with peer groups.
6. Taking responsibility for your own life and working hard for your own goals.
7. Identifying inappropriate defence mechanisms and having the courage to give them up through counselling or other means of self help.

## EXPLORING THE IMPORTANCE OF EMOTIONAL COMPETENCE

There are many ways in which emotional competence can be defined as important and it would be difficult to decide if one was more important than another. It is not always helpful to try and separate out specific areas as we are looking at achieving a life which is an overall success for ourselves and our children.

## Maintaining relationships

If we do not know how to relate to ourselves, how can we relate to each other and build the relationships which fulfil our emotional needs and enrich our lives, either at work or at home? Communications are the basis of all relationships and the effectiveness of communications decides the quality and cohesiveness of the relationship. The relationships we all have with each other create small social groups, which collect to form the larger group we call society. Thus if we all improve our own relationship with ourselves, then with each other, we then have the potential to build a better society.

## Social implications

Society is made up of individuals and we are all part of it. The overview of society is a summary of what we are all saying, thinking, feeling and doing. Nothing happens without some sort of thought process and the governing influences of those thoughts are emotions and emotional experiences. Although logic is a formative basis for thought, the final response always comes from emotional reactions.

We cannot separate ourselves from society because it reflects us all. We cannot expect anyone to take responsibility for anyone else. We create our own reality through the subjective perceptual experience of society. For some it is full of potential and yet others perceive it as doom and gloom, with all the shades in between. It is the same society but the only difference is the perceptual viewpoint of the individual. One person's disaster is another's opportunity. Nothing else differs, only the perception and the history of emotions behind that interpretation. Thus Jane may see the ending of the relationship with Keith as a new beginning. She may recognise what she has learned from the relationship, or she could feel as if she is a victim deserted by yet another male. The choice is hers but it will affect her whole future. It is an emotional choice.

There is an increasing recognition of social problems and debate over whose responsibility it is to sort it all out. We are all aware of rising violence in society and even children of five are demonstrating a capacity for considerable violence against each other. Clearly we are not talking about the normal rough and tumble of childhood, rather like the playful tangle of puppies or kittens that teach them certain skills and tests their strength.

But this is not the only crisis in our society. There are more relationship breakdowns, children taken into care, failures within the academic system, increased dependency on the state, dependency on chemicals, nervous breakdown and mental health problems, a growing phenomenon of incidental violence such as road rage and random mass killings – for example, Dunblane. This is all to do with a lack of emotional competence in society and in individuals.

*Why we need emotional competence*
The reasons we need to develop emotional competence are:

- developing and maintaining close intimate relationships
- taking responsibility for our own emotions and behaviour
- reducing stress in our lives
- enabling clear expression of needs, thoughts and feelings
- improving mental and physical health
- enabling learning to take place, both academic and social, without fear
- achieving one's potential
- creating a happier and more peaceful society.

None of us can take responsibility for others in achieving the above, as adults and parents we must do it for ourselves. Then we can begin to rear a generation of children who have the emotional competence to create just that society.

## LEARNING TOGETHER

The most important point to make here is that **we are all doing the best we can with what we know**. Understanding this is the third step to emotional competence. There is rarely any exception to this rule unless someone clearly does know what they are doing and is conscious of their bad behaviour. In a sense even they are doing their best because they have yet to learn that there are better ways of getting the results they seek without resorting to violence, bullying, unkindness etc.

Keith could have ensured Megan's love for him in many other

ways, but he had not learned to trust other people. He believed that he had to manipulate her in order to protect himself and her love for him, as his father taught him and treated him. He was doing the best he could for himself with what he knew, and in many ways he intended the best for Megan too, from his point of view. Since he could not trust anyone, neither should she. He was teaching her the only self protection he knew. Every time it failed him, as with the breakdown of so many relationships and job changes, this was evidence for him of how right he was not to allow himself to trust anyone and openly say what he felt and thought.

### Avoiding learning

The kind of stress produced by such inner conflict has long been associated with self pity and depression. The biggest barrier to learning is fear of change. However much we complain about things, most people do not want to change. They want someone else to do so instead. Yet the courage to make that change results in a very different life. Getting it wrong first enables us to appreciate how good it really can be when you embrace the learning process.

### Parenting – a new learning opportunity

Having children represents a need for continuous change; from confirmation of the pregnancy onwards, parents have options:

- They can resist change and make the experience as difficult for each other as possible.
- They can predict change and try to control the process.
- They can be open to the new experiences and learn new emotional responses as they arise.

Your children will represent many opportunities for you to change yourself too. Children act as mirrors of ourselves and we as parents need to look closely to see what is being reflected back to us.

### Understanding mirroring

If we recognise that children can teach us much about ourselves, we can learn from them and teach them what we have learned. They act as mirrors. If there is something they do which we find uncomfortable, it is likely it is a reflection of you. With young children especially, where else has that behaviour come from? Learn from their simple demonstration of you and accept the opportunity. If you feel angry, take time to reflect and work through the exercise above. Consider the root cause of that response. You do not have to like your children but if you don't, you probably don't like yourself and they probably won't like you either. Are they too similar to you for comfort? Only you can change that.

Several dramatic assumptions are made in this chapter about parenting. Make a list of all the arguments you have now and tuck them into the cover of the book. Hopefully they will all be discussed as the book progresses. Parenting has never been easy, so don't expect a book about parenting skills to be easy either.

**SUMMARY**

Parents can:

- identify emotions and their root causes
- recognise that they have choices of how to respond to experiences
- learn how to use empathy for the good of the other and not for oneself
- define success
- identify their opportunities for learning
- identify the significance, for the individual and for society, of emotional competence
- accept that we are **all** doing our best with what we know
- understand and value mirroring from their child, recognising their own need for learning.

# 2
# Parenting Skills and Styles: Teacher or Hypocrite

## EVOLVING PARENTING SKILLS

We are not born with parenting skills and they do not come with puberty or in a neat package of instructions on arrival with the first child. They reflect our emotions and communication skills and our need to evolve as the child develops and changes.

Parenting skills can be learned through recognition of how we think, feel and behave towards our children. Parents with more than one child will probably recognise that they use different skills with different children, in accordance with:

- age
- gender
- relationship styles
- personality
- interactions within the family
- other factors within the extended family
- social/environmental factors
- resources, both material and emotional.

There is no easy stage in parenting either. They all present challenges and opportunities for learning. As parents we evolve with our children.

Before the child is born parents have experiences and assumptions which form a theoretical starting point for the work ahead:

- own childhood experiences
- observation of sibling childhood experiences
- own parents' styles and approaches

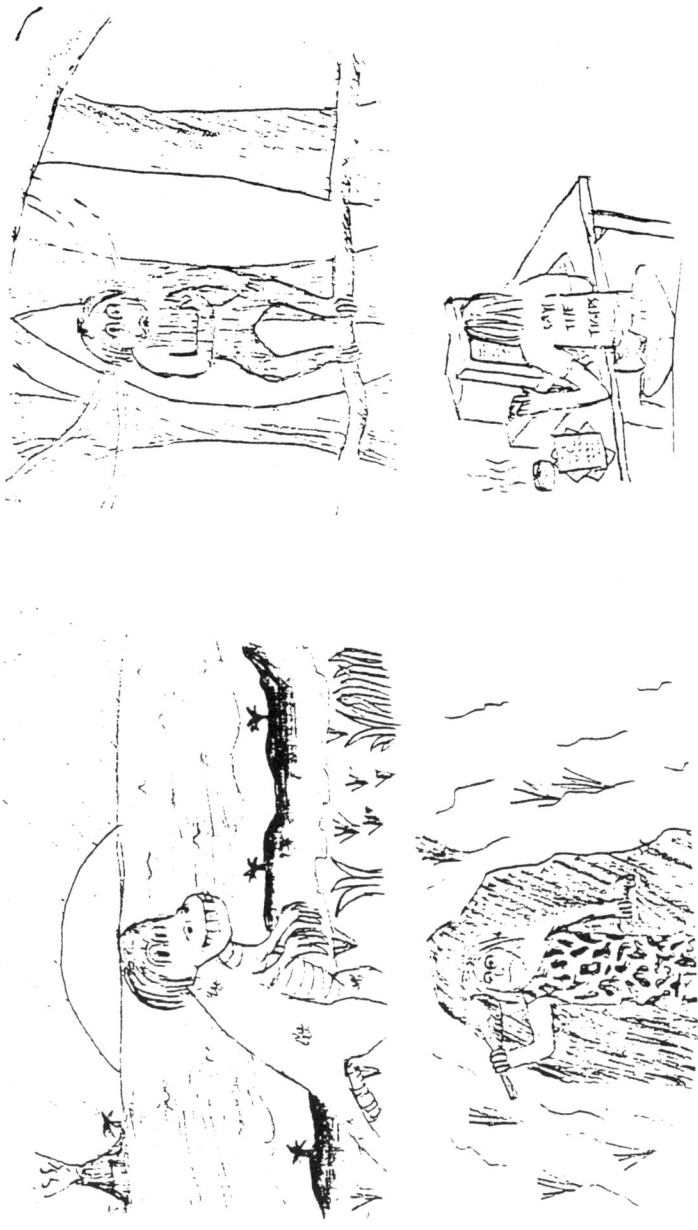

Fig. 3. The Evolution of Mums by Ben Cole

First we have the mumosaurus, a peaceful herbivore
Next we have the mumkey, who carried her children everywhere with her
Then comes the early humum who likes to leave the cave and go off hunting herself

- parents' relationship with grandparents
- advice from books and experts
- observation of others around you
- media influences and attitudes
- extended family value systems
- peer groups.

## LEARNING LESSONS

As parents, we are learning lessons and children are the best teachers. Through them we have the opportunity to revisit our own childhood experiences, gaining perspectives that differ from the view held as a child. Many new parents turn to their own mothers and fathers and say that they now understand the difficulties their parents faced. This is a time for healing old arguments and developing new relationships as adults and equals, with experiences of parenting in common.

### Recognising good and bad lessons

We have all learned parenting skills from our own parents. These can take two forms:

1. We can recognise things we appreciate from our childhood and pass examples of good practice on to our children. This is an opportunity to appreciate our positive experiences.
2. We can recognise difficult areas and use this as 'a lesson in how not to do it'. This means taking a negative experience and making it positive for the present and the future.

Our own childhood, however hard, is the most valuable resource for developing parenting skills. Above all it is important to recognise that, whether our own childhood felt predominantly good or bad, it was the making of us. We can never change that, but we can use those valuable lessons to their fullest advantage with our own children.

### Perpetuating damaging parenting experiences

Too often adults who have had difficult experiences in childhood are still too angry with their own parents to see the value of those experiences. That anger will affect our children and result in perpetuating our experiences through our parenting skills. Keith is passing his fear on to his daughter. He lives with a model of a frightened, rejected little boy inside and is responding with that child's emotions. His inner child is damaged and without healing himself, the damage is perpetuated.

## Healing the inner child

Antenatal lessons should be less about how to feed the baby and more about how to heal your inner child and release negative experiences so that your child can benefit from your lessons. You will benefit by releasing old negative emotions and re-creating a positive childhood experience. This should be done regularly because as your child grows, unresolved issues from different stages through your own childhood re-awake.

The best way to identify these is to think about what creates a strong emotional response, good or bad. Use exercise 1.1 to identify those emotions and their source. When you have done that, you are ready to start the healing process.

There are two exercises which can help this process.

## Exercise 2.1

This requires that you think about your bad experiences first.

- Write a list of your principal areas of difficulty, then choose one to work on. You can work through the rest later.

- Look at what those experiences taught you. This is **what you had to be** to cope with the decisions that your parents made. Are you, for instance, determined, assertive, gentle, kind, independent? Did you work hard at school to prove them wrong? Did you become passive, quiet, easily content? Look for positive outcomes, wherever they are.

All experiences develop active and passive behaviours as survival skills. Active responses are confrontational, rejecting, fighting skills. Passive responses are the areas where we yielded, learned compromise, and peace-keeping skills. All have their value and everyone has a different balance.

- How do those skills and qualities benefit us now?
- Is there any other way that your parents could have taught this?

- What would your life be like now if you had not developed this ability or quality?
- Are you still angry with your parents; do you need to be?

**Exercise 2.2**
Find a photograph of yourself as a young child and look yourself in the eye. Recognise all the courage and strength, all the ingenuity that this child needed in order to get to where you are now. Tell that child how much you empathise with all their difficulties and how well they've done with what they knew. Send that child messages of love, daily.

**Resisting resistance**
Quite probably as you work through these exercises you will find a reluctance to adopt these new perspectives because it means that all those problems which caused you so much grief were actually good for you. This does not mean that the experiences were good, or that we were 'wrong' or 'bad' children and deserved them.

The past continues to hurt only if we let it. Releasing negative childhood experiences is central to developing successful parenting skills which ensure a successful future for your child. Children are like sponges, they absorb our emotional energies and adopt our emotional patterns. An angry or frightened parent will produce an angry or frightened child, either actively or passively demonstrating the reflection. If we are still angry and hurt by our own childhood experiences we are passing that on to our children.

## EXPLORING THE POWER IN PARENTING

All relationships have a power element, based on who makes the decisions and sets the agenda, whose values are the dominant ones and who takes responsibility. With a young baby the parents have total power. Balance is established by parents who give the child a degree of power over them.

A good example of this is how parents respond to a crying child:

1. They always rush to the attention of a crying child, giving the child the power to summon mum or dad whenever they wish.
2. They never respond quickly at all; they are clearly in total control and leaving the child feeling very helpless and powerless.

3. They respond to the child without appearing to rush to their every whim, demonstrating to the infant that their needs are recognised and their expressions of distress and need for attention are respected, but not above all else.

The balance of power continues to vary and develop throughout your relationship.

### Assessing power relationships

Assess the power balance in the relationships around you by answering the following questions:

1. How much time do you spend reflecting on a request or comment from your child?
2. How quickly do you respond to your child's demands?
3. Do you give answers to requests without discussion?
4. Do you take time to consider how important this request is to your child?
5. Do you give your child full attention while discussing their request?

Answering questions like these is an opportunity for you to reflect and consider what you are currently doing and if this is or is not the intention that you have. With children over about seven years of age it might be interesting to ask them to answer these questions about you as a parent. Then you can see if your intentions are what is experienced by your child.

## LEARNING BY EXAMPLE

Understanding how society functions is learned by observing those around us. Our first role models are close family members, and their behaviours are the ones which get copied and mirrored back. The more people your child comes into contact with, the better range of role models they have to choose from. Childminders and extended family influences, nursery school teachers and peers all provide each child with the range of options. It is often possible to see one behaviour adopted from one source member and another from elsewhere. Equally they are rejecting alternatives from everyone else. Thus children show discernment from a very early age.

### Imitating skills of young children

How often do we see ourselves through the eyes of our child, aspects that we prefer not to see? This mirroring is a wonderful opportunity to examine our own behaviours and take note of the type of model we are providing. If you dislike something that your child does it is probably because you dislike or fear something similar in yourself. How do you respond in these situations:

- Do you become angry or irritated by the child?
- Do you consider what this is telling you about yourself?
- Do you ignore them and hope it will go away?

It is pointless becoming angry with the child for their behaviour if you are the original model for them. If it is copied from someone else and you dislike it, consider why this is so. Make sure that it is not your own agenda which is influencing you. Discuss the influence and its merits with your child, and offer them alternatives so that they can choose which role model to adopt. Having found a comfortable one for themselves, they will then adopt it as a norm of their own behaviour patterns.

It can take some time to reprogramme behaviour, but is achievable once we have openly and honestly acknowledged our need to change. The most positive response is to **recognise the opportunity to change** your own behaviour, and thereby provide a role model that your child would value.

Parents often underestimate the impression their own efforts to change make on their children. This is also providing an excellent role model in itself because it gives children permission to try things out and make changes. The meta-message is **change is good**.

### Fearing change

Fear of change is the biggest block to emotional competence. Yet work done in therapy and personal development does achieve change in ways which enhance the inner self and peel away the negative behaviours which are the result of fear. Many adults experience considerable fear of change and will resist it to quite extraordinary degrees, until the change is forced upon them in ways that are painful and dramatic. Some may choose to live a safe life that avoids challenges and achieves little. If your intention is to raise a successful child, then neither of these options will support that goal. Look back to Maslow's characteristics of self actualisers (page 22) to see how many of these you hold.

### Valuing children's mistakes

All children make mistakes. All adults make mistakes. Everyone fails to achieve something at first and it is the process of trying that allows us to succeed a few attempts down the line. Having also failed first we know how to avoid further pitfalls. Failing first is essential for thorough learning to take place.

Children need to have all their attempts valued, not just the successful ones. It is the process that counts, not the final outcome, and if we only praise the successful outcome we undervalue the process it took to get there. One of the keys to success in professional, academic and social emotional life is valuing the process and using it as a positive learning opportunity. By valuing it we do not retreat from difficulty and remain open to the process of growth.

## RECOGNISING HIDDEN AGENDAS IN PARENTING

Whether we like it or not, most people are experts in games of hidden agendas because most families play them to a degree. They vary enormously in severity and often follow the type of communication patterns of Jane, Megan and Keith. The main point to remember here is that they all have a hidden or secondary gain other than the expressed intention and use dishonest communication styles and double binds. As with most aspects of parenting, in order to avoid teaching your child the same styles, you must look at your communication patterns and hidden agendas.

### Using children to gain love

One of the fundamental needs for all humans is to feel loved but we can only receive that which we also give out. Keith needs love and uses his daughter and others to fulfil that need. He does not give love and receive it in return, he extracts it.

Babies are experts at giving out love, which they need to receive as care and survival. They are totally dependent on their parents, even if they are being abused. In order to receive, babies give. They already know this rule and give endless uncritical and forgiving love. It has no hidden agendas. It is a means to survival as a human being and this is a fundamental truth for all of us.

Babies are born with this capacity and it is childhood experience which teaches them differently. If, as a parent, you already have unconditional love why do you need to distort your child's love by manipulating it, like Megan and Keith?

> **You receive what you give out and you give out what you have learned.**

If you have had a lack of love in your own childhood, your insecurity will make it hard for you to trust and rely on the lasting quality of the love from your child. If our emotional well is empty, no matter how much love our child gives us, it will never be enough. Only we can learn how to fill it for ourselves. Your child can only be inadequate in meeting your needs and will learn to perceive themselves in this way. Your need to be loved as a parent will create in your child a sense of failure.

Having favourites is even more destructive to the child concerned because of the pressure upon them to give the parent a reward in return for the position on the pedestal. The favoured child becomes isolated from siblings and locked into an impossible need fulfilment mission for the favouring parent. Who is taking care of the child's needs?

### Using children to gain a sense of power

In much of our adult life we seem to have little power. As children this may feel even more true. There are always people who have more authority, more muscles, more money, more of whatever it is that appears to give them power. In the end these are just illusions. The true power comes from inner knowledge and strength, from a sense of integrity, knowing what your boundaries are, what you will and will not do, or allow others to do to you. It comes from understanding that all the behaviour of others is their responsibility and not yours.

### CASE STUDY

### Megan feels needlessly guilty

Megan tells Keith that she wants to see Jane and Sam. This makes Keith very insecure and he expresses this as anger. Megan sees how distressed her father is and feels guilty about it. She decides not to see them any more. Keith then apologises to Megan and tells her not to talk about Jane and Sam any more because of how they have treated him. Megan is left feeling that she was wrong to bring up the subject.

## Using your child to protect yourself

If we as parents lose our temper and behave badly as a result, then justify this by indirectly telling the child they are to blame for having upset us, this is using the child to protect us from our own unresolved emotions. As parents we can wield power over our children in a number of ways:

- by making decisions for them
- by denying them the right to make mistakes
- by making them feel guilty for upsetting us
- by denying their right for a degree of autonomy in their own lives.

If we lack a sense of autonomy in our own lives, we feel powerless. One of the ways in which we can make ourselves feel more powerful is to use the models of power that other people use over us. If we do that then we are passing on our own sense of inadequacy to our child. We can never feel powerful in our own lives if we do not recognise our powerlessness first and acknowledge our strength in that honesty. If we use our children's lives as an exercise in regaining power in our own we are abusing our child and teaching them that they too are powerless. By removing their sense of power you also remove their sense of potential and redirect the energy they need in order to achieve their goals into the desire to fill the need for autonomy in their lives. We empower ourselves by accepting our limitations and working with them to develop ourselves and to achieve anyway.

## Wanting to be God

Some parents try to be the superhuman, the ideal that they wish they could be and that perhaps their parents also created an illusion of. The trouble with being God is that eventually your child will notice that you are not and this will confuse, disillusion and ultimately undermine the very esteem and respect upon which their love is based.

In playing God you are also denying them the right to be special in their own way. There can only be one God. However, they will probably spend the rest of their lives looking for someone to treat them like God. They may fail at relationships because their ideals are too high and based on fear of not being God, of not being as good as their parents. The honest parent who makes honest mistakes teaches their child to love others as equal humans and most of all to love themselves as a less than perfect human. If we want to be God then we are also certainly feeling very inadequate inside and are struggling to hide it from everyone, including ourselves.

## Using children to feel needed

In modern Western society the apprenticeship for adulthood lasts well beyond attaining adult physical status. The more complex a society is, the harder it is for the individual to be truly independent and indeed none of us is. We all need each other but there is a difference between dependency and interdependence. The latter is acceptable because it implies a quality of independence.

We all need to have our own sense of direction. Unfortunately many parents see their children's needs as their own identity, their value in society. If it is a choice to have children then allow the child to develop in their own direction. Deciding unilaterally what is best for your child is meeting your own needs for your child to show you up well in society, to enhance your social standing. Making sacrifices or staying at home to care for your children, and demonstrating a lack of direction when they no longer need you, puts pressure on them to continue to be dependent. Children should never feel beholden to their parents and a healthy respect and affection will carry the relationship through into old age.

## SUMMARY

- Parenting skills are learned on the job but are also based on a range of influences. Awareness of these allows conscious choice.
- Our own childhood was the making of us and it is our responsibility to make that a positive outcome.
- Recognise the power roles in parenting and balance them for the child's developing sense of autonomy.
- Recognise the mirroring of ourselves by our children and use this as an opportunity to change.
- Accept the fact of hidden agendas in parenting and diffuse them through recognition and self healing.

# 3
# Prioritising for Parents

The chances are that, if you are reading this book, your children are your priority – bringing them up with a good start in life, keeping them safe until they are old enough to be independent.

It is important to keep in mind that generally there is no right or wrong way to parent. Eighty per cent of parents get it right more or less and each style of parenting teaches your child something. Sometimes the outcome isn't what we expected and this can make it harder for your child to be successful, but that is part of the learning experience. It is how we address our mistakes that really counts.

Are your children your priority or not? Do you really know what your priorities are? Does anyone? Before you disagree with this question please take time to consider the following questions.

## ASSESSING PRIORITIES

What are the most important areas of your own life? Please number the list below in order of importance for you. Take time to reflect before you complete this.

Look at each of the areas listed a–k below and decide if there are any others you should add for your own life. Now consider each area in the following way:

- How much time and effort do you put into each of the areas, how much thought and planning, how much energy?
- What proportion of your waking time do you spend actively in each area of your life?
- Of course at work you have to think about work, but do you think about other areas of your life during the day?
- Do you find yourself thinking about work when you are at home with your family?
- Are you working for the family or for your work?

By applying these criteria to each of the areas listed you can assess your priorities. Use a 1–5 scale with 1 = high priority and 5 = low priority.

(a)  relationships with spouse/partner
(b)  relationship with child/ren
(c)  relationships with friends
(d)  relationships at work
(e)  success at work
(f)  material comfort and status
(g)  social image and reputation
(h)  feeling at peace with yourself and your conscience
(i)  winning or excelling at something
(j)  winning approval from other people however you can
(k)  your own priority.

It is useful to carry out this exercise for yourself and your co-parent and to compare your perceived priorities with how they are perceived by those around you. What does this tell you about your priorities? How balanced are the areas of your life? And how does your score compare with your partner's view of you and vice versa?

The closer your score compares to your partner's score, the more in tune you are with each other – a good sign for consistency at least, but let's explore a little further. If you are in tune you are also likely to be very conscious of your priorities and choose how to spend your time and energy quite carefully. If your scores differ considerably, where does this occur? This exercise does not have right or wrong answers and is another way of exploring your present position with yourself and your life.

## PRIORITISING CHILDREN

Apply the same assessment procedure on behalf of your children, using the next list. It is helpful to do a comparison list with your co-parent here too.

(a)  relationships with siblings
(b)  relationships with parents
(c)  relationships with friends
(d)  relationships at work
(e)  success at work
(f)  material comfort and status
(g)  social image and reputation

(h) feeling at peace with themselves and their conscience
(i) winning or excelling at something
(j) winning approval from other people, especially parents, however they can
(k) their own priority.

How do these lists equate with each other? If your child is old enough, ask them to complete this list and compare your lists with those of your child. The closer your lists are to each other the more likely you are to succeed in the parenting, learning process.

### Understanding our priorities
We gradually develop priorities by acknowledging our needs. These include material and physiological needs for the maintenance of life, emotional needs, esteem needs, social needs and intellectual needs. Abraham Maslow described these as a hierarchy, which he represented in two sections, basic or 'deficiency' needs, and 'being' needs (see Figure 3).

It is now argued that they are of equal significance, and that, for instance, we can meet levels three and four without level one being met. Maslow acknowledged that many role models for his theory of self actualisation were quite unhappy in other areas of their life. They had to sacrifice one area in order to achieve in another. An emotionally competent adult can actively develop themselves well enough to achieve and maintain a successful balance in all aspects of their life.

## BALANCING NEEDS

Although these needs are common to all humans, it is the balance between them which is affected by our childhood and life experiences. Childhood creates the mould and experiences are interpreted to confirm this sense of reality. Thus if experience places material needs as a higher order priority than intellectual needs, that will become our priority for adult life.

## CASE STUDY

### John and Michele strive to please their parents
Mike and Mary have two children, aged four and six. They both work full time and the family lives in a spacious home with every comfort. They have an excellent trained nanny and both children

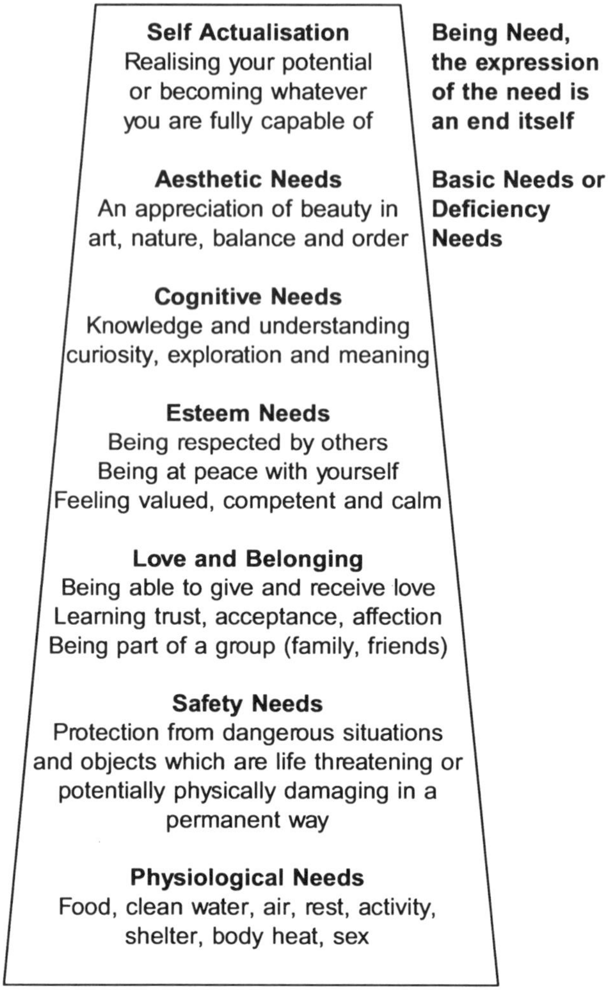

**Self Actualisation**
Realising your potential
or becoming whatever
you are fully capable of

**Being Need,
the expression
of the need is
an end itself**

**Aesthetic Needs**
An appreciation of beauty in
art, nature, balance and order

**Basic Needs or
Deficiency
Needs**

**Cognitive Needs**
Knowledge and understanding
curiosity, exploration and meaning

**Esteem Needs**
Being respected by others
Being at peace with yourself
Feeling valued, competent and calm

**Love and Belonging**
Being able to give and receive love
Learning trust, acceptance, affection
Being part of a group (family, friends)

**Safety Needs**
Protection from dangerous situations
and objects which are life threatening or
potentially physically damaging in a
permanent way

**Physiological Needs**
Food, clean water, air, rest, activity,
shelter, body heat, sex

There is quite a lot of discussion about the relevance of this model but it is a useful way to look at the range of needs we all have. Self actualisation is the highest of these needs. It is seen as being the highest level of attainment and the higher up the hierarchy you get the harder it is to achieve. Maslow identified qualities which he considered part of self actualisation, although it is all a question of degree. (See Chapter 1.)

Fig. 3. The hierarchy of needs.
Abraham Maslow (1954)

attend private prep school. At weekends the whole family goes to a sports centre for coaching lessons in a range of sports. After the lessons they all go for a family meal and sit around a table discussing the achievement and progress each of them have made.

The children also have a number of after-school activities such as music lessons and both are expected to practise regularly. They are not praised for their achievement but are continuously coached to 'get better' at everything. The parents are both very proud of the success of their parenting strategy and recognise the competence of each child already, to each other. They are reluctant to praise their children too much in case it makes them too complacent in their achievement.

John and Michele work very hard at trying to please their precious parents. They rarely see them and they are often reminded how hard Mum and Dad both work to provide them with all of the goods things they have in life. They feel guilty if they cannot show some progress each week as a reward for their parents. They do not enjoy their activities and are laden with responsibility to succeed. They both feel inadequate because they are unable to meet their parents' high expectations sufficiently in order to get the praise which they see their friends receiving from their parents – for what seems to be much less. They both already feel that somehow they must be woefully inadequate in ways that neither can understand.

Twenty years on, Mike and Mary tell all their friends how proud they are of both of their children in their academic records and professional achievement. They are hoping that eventually one of them will find a steady partner and settle down and provide them with grandchildren too. At the moment neither seems able to keep a partner for long, there's always something 'wrong' with them. And they are concerned that already John has high blood pressure and Michele has irritable bowel syndrome. These are both stress-related conditions. Mike feels that they should find a good family life like they had when they were young, in order to cope with the stress and help them to relax.

- What have John and Michele been taught about themselves and their intrinsic value?
- Was this what their parents intended?
- What did the parents intend to show their children?
- What adjustment could they have made to their parenting style which would have made a difference?

- Which parenting skill are they demonstrating a lack of?
- Both parents identify an area of failure in their children's lives: where do they look for the explanation of this?

### Acknowledging your own mistakes

Consider your answers to these questions carefully and look for any areas of your own parenting skills which might be similarly falling short. Honestly acknowledge it and forgive yourself for making a mistake first, so that you do not make your child more laden with guilt and responsibility for forgiving you and making you feel better. Simply tell your child that you are getting it wrong, and that you will attempt to get it right in the future. They will feel much better for this and will have more respect for you for being honest and human. It means that they are allowed to get it wrong too, if you can.

### Addressing the priorities

Whether your children are your priorities or not, it is how you address those priorities that needs to be considered. Protecting your child can mean that inadvertently we do the opposite. If we do all the protecting, how can our child learn how to protect themselves? We can control some of their environment and experiences and obviously protect them from life-threatening situations, but the more we strive for control the more impossible it becomes. Both parent and child become involved in a major power battle over who is controlling whose life. If you do not allow your child to take risks and face difficult situations, they will either withdraw completely and be quite unable to face anything or they will become high risk takers, and rebellious, to prove their independence.

### Accepting changes

In reality our priorities change and grow as the circumstances change around us. The flexibility to change our priorities in response to the changes around us is also an essential life skill. This is one of the most important lessons that we all have to learn in order to achieve the balance which brings inner peace and success, the elements of emotional intelligence: keeping a sense of perspective on everything at all times and responding flexibly to maintain the balance. This balance is achieved by learning the lessons which bring us to that understanding.

# Prioritising for Parents

## SUMMARY

- Priorities are important to assess for parents and for children.
- Co-parents can examine and refine their priorities to be in tune with each other.
- Children should be allowed to develop their own priorities.
- Remain flexible to the changes in needs and priorities of children through different ages.

# 4
# Avoiding the Over-Protection Trap

**MAKING MISTAKES IS ESSENTIAL**

As pointed out by many child psychologists and philosophers, in the first half of this century parents wondered **if** their child would grow up. Now we worry about **how** our child will grow up. This chapter re-addresses some of the points in previous chapters and takes them a little further.

**Assessing the importance of making mistakes**
Think about times which taught you the most important lessons in your own life, and the events which sparked off that greatest period of learning. I am talking about life lessons: the kind that teach you about other people and most of all teach you about yourself. I expect most learning and advancement occurred in terms of self knowledge, and of other people and life generally, at a time of great inner struggle. The most difficult experiences are usually our best teachers, if we let them be. The more we fight to hide, the more they come and find us. They are essential to continuing growth and development.

- What were the most important lessons that you learned in your life? Please list a few here. What kind of lessons have you listed? I hope you listed things about:

  | | | |
  |---|---|---|
  | love | forgiveness | prosperity |
  | health | friendship | empathy |
  | generosity | honesty | knowledge |
  | creativity | joy | respect |
  | patience | compassion | communication |
  | trust | responsibility | intuition |

These are important lessons because they relate to other people and to our knowledge of ourselves. If we do not explore ourselves as parents, we cannot teach our children to have a healthy outlook and sense of self. We can forgive and release negative experiences in the same way as the inner child healing exercise. Work through the following questions and give yourself time to consider your responses.

- Was there any other way that you could have learned those lessons as thoroughly?
- Was there anyone who could have told you about those lessons and saved you the experience?
- Would you have listened?

Please answer these questions as you remember feeling **before** you went through the experience and before the wisdom and learning occurred. **Do not** use the wisdom of hindsight.

## LEARNING LESSONS IN SIX DIMENSIONS

Some lessons appear to be easier than others, but in reality they are not, for each lesson has to be learned in a six-way direction (see Figure 4). It cannot happen all at once. Each lesson is learned in a series of many little steps or a couple of big and very tough ones. The harder the lesson, the greater the potential for learning – a new interpretation for 'no pain, no gain'. The more quickly we learn these lessons the more quickly we advance in our emotional intelligence.

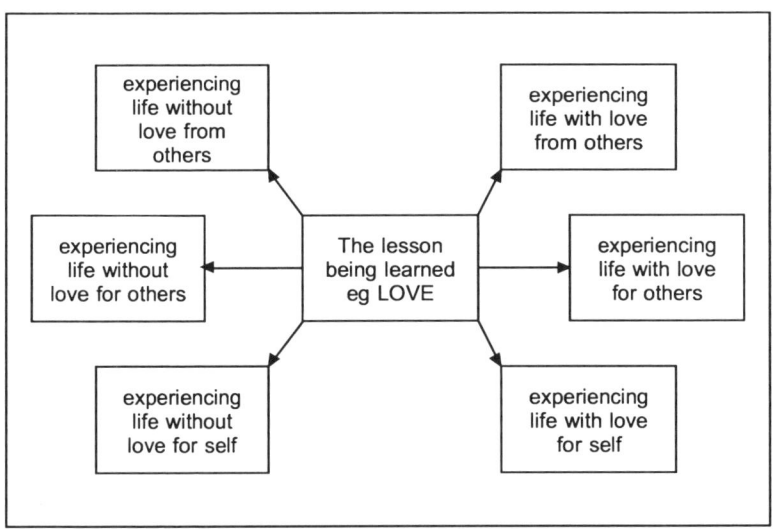

Fig. 4. Directions of learning.

### Dealing with traumatic experiences

There are two ways of dealing with traumatic experiences. The first is to become damaged, to see yourself as the victim, to retreat from any situation which might similarly challenge you. This is negative learning which increases fear and life avoidance. Before continuing, answer yes or no to the questions below:

- Are there any areas of your life where the lessons were so hard that you have withdrawn to any degree from that part of your life?
- Have your withdrawals been temporary or permanent?
- Do you desire success in that area of your life in spite of it all?
- Do you feel confused by why it never seems to go right?
- Does someone else always seem to mess it up by not doing what you want them to do?

If you have answered yes to any of the above, and if we're at all honest there will be at least one area of our own lives where YES is the truthful answer, then you've still got a few lessons to learn in that area.

### Learning the lessons as they are presented to us

As adults, we actually frequently revisit experiences in different formats. Take one of the lessons such as trust. Figure 4 shows the six dimensions to learning a life lesson. We have to learn each of the six dimensions in trust to fully understand it and live in harmony with it.

## CASE STUDY

### Jane repeats childhood experience

As a young girl Jane was repeatedly beaten by her father for being naughty. She didn't understand why because he never bothered to explain it to her. But she knew that her father was big and she depended on him for everything so he must be right. She learned to try very hard to always get things right and to please her father. She learned to associate love with fear. As she grew older she learned that her father might actually be wrong. She also realised that her father was scared of being wrong. This gave her a sense of power over him, a redress of the unfair balance of power she experienced as a young girl. As she reaches adulthood she learns that she can use guilt and fear to make her father give her what she wants. He can't hit her any more but he can now use money to keep her love. Jane then gets married. After three years her husband hits her for challenging him. He feels guilty and begs forgiveness. Jane forgives him and he takes her out to buy some new clothes. She can choose whatever she likes. They agree to have a child and she becomes pregnant. Jane is stuck in the continuing cycle until she can learn all the lessons from the negative side.

We cannot understand love and trust until we have learned to be without it, and we cannot understand living without fear until we have learned to live with it. It is the negative side which teaches us the value of the positive side.

## PROTECTING OR INHIBITING

### Accepting the lessons

Young people who experienced a traumatic or violent childhood will commonly repeat those mistakes and find similar adult partners. If they haven't fully explored the experiences of that childhood with an open and gentle learning approach, they will not have learned the lessons they need.

If we as children had experience of similar parenting to that identified above, or a variation, we can choose to learn from that experience.

- We can choose how not to parent using fear as a control of our children's love for us.

- We can learn from the mistakes of our parents and those traumatic experiences in a very important way because we know exactly how it feels to live with that kind of parenting.

- We have the choice – to continue to live like that ourselves or to choose an alternative.

The important thing about difficult experiences is the learning we receive. By denying difficult experiences a child cannot test their strength, learn and understand in their own way. If you deny them learning in their early years they will have to re-experience them later and their ability to handle and manage their adulthood is undermined. If you put off the lesson, it will be learned later and with longer lasting consequences, especially if you haven't got the coping skills which childhood should have provided you with.

So if you're not providing your child with those experiences within the family, they will have to confront them somewhere else.

## CASE STUDY

### Jane prevents Sam from coping

Jane has started working again after leaving her violent ex-husband. She enjoys the work and tells Sam, her twelve-year-old son, that he must travel home from school alone. This is fine for eight months, he enjoys the freedom. One day, as he gets off the bus near his home, he is attacked by a gang of slightly older boys from his school. He is physically injured, mostly cuts and bruises, and is shaken by the experience. Jane is upset and shocked. She feels guilty that she enjoys working and made him travel alone. She hushes him whenever he starts to show his upset. She tells him that it was all wrong, that people shouldn't treat him like that and he didn't deserve it. It will never happen again.

The physical injuries heal quickly. She rearranges her work time to allow her to leave a little earlier. From now on she collects him either from school or from the bus stop every day, to make sure that it will never happen again and to show her son how much she loves him. She tells herself and everyone else that she is protecting her adolescent son from the possibility of this recurring.

Having read this case study, now try to answer these questions:

- Who is Jane protecting and from what?
- How does Sam feel when next faced by a similar experience in school?
- What lessons has Sam learned from this experience?
- Is Jane protecting her son from the possibility of an attack or herself from the guilt she feels from his first attack?

Jane feels that somehow she should have protected him and it shouldn't have happened. He shouldn't have been exposed to that violence.

Why not? All through life we are on the receiving end of attacks from other people. Sometimes they are physical and sometimes they are emotional, psychological or spiritual. How do we deal with them? Are we injured by them or do we see them as someone else's problem? There are many ways of coping with assaults on our integrity whether it is physical or psychological; but without the

# Avoiding the Over-Protection Trap

experiences to learn from, we do not know what our coping skills are. We do not know how to survive and we become damaged.

Sam's physical cuts and bruises only took a couple of weeks to heal but the emotional healing will take much longer until it is addressed as an opportunity to learn from. If Jane feels guilty about 'letting it happen', she will transfer that guilt to Sam. But he will understand that he caused his mother's guilt, and therefore accept responsibility. He feels ashamed of the assault by not being allowed to talk about it. Somehow he must be asking for it.

- What coping skills has Sam been able to develop?

My answer to this last question is 'To let someone else deal with it and protect him'. Is this a lesson of any use at all? Is this a lesson that will enable Sam to deal with other forms of attack later in life? It's important not to become judgmental here but to allow that we, as parents, are also allowed to make mistakes and learn our lessons. As I said in Chapters 1 and 2, children tend to respect their parents more for not getting it right all the time.

- What would you feel if Sam were your child?
- What would you automatically want to do?
- Whose needs would you be addressing?
- Whose needs should you really be addressing?

> **There are no mistakes, only lessons to be learned.**

It would be a good idea to introduce this as a daily pause for thought for everyone. We would all make progress in our lives if we were not so afraid of learning lessons by getting it wrong first.

## PUTTING OFF THE LESSONS

Jane is putting off the lessons Sam must learn. Many people would think it best under the circumstances. What would any of us do in similar circumstances with our own children? Well, it has happened to my son too. And it was scary for me to let him go out again to the same road and the same situation. I probably lost half a stone that night. But his self confidence grew by not being protected. He learned to walk confidently through the streets and assume responsibility for his own safety.

There is much evidence, especially on street rape and assault, that it is less likely to happen to people who walk confidently. The rapist or bully does not enjoy the violence but they want the sense of power for boosting their own sense of powerlessness. By preventing your child from being confident in themselves and undermining their ability to cope, you place them at greater risk. Now consider these questions carefully:

- Is Jane really protecting Sam from the chance of another attack or is she increasing the likelihood?
- How is Sam's self concept and perception developing, as victim or independent young man?
- What other choices are there for dealing with a situation like this?

### Teaching a child to learn from this kind of experience

Such an experience can undermine self esteem but there are ways of approaching this:

- Help the child to face their fear of a recurrence by looking at what the experience has already taught them.
- What were their emotional reactions as the experience progressed? Discuss in depth exactly how everything that happened affected them and talk it through. Nothing is unacceptable.
- Help them to see what the lessons are.
- Teach them about the victim/bully attitude system.

Being on the receiving end of violence may be something that they can think about. In the future if they are tempted to attack someone, this experience reminds them what it feels like at the other end. Would they want to make someone feel as they felt? If they ever lose their temper, that can be what it feels like on the other side. Or what it might feel like for someone else whom they observe being bullied. It is an important lesson in empathy. This experience is not a disaster, it is an important opportunity for learning – painful but valuable. So don't hush it up, use it, milk it for all the learning possible.

### Controlling what you can and leaving the rest

You cannot control the environment and experience and any fear or

## Avoiding the Over-Protection Trap

failure you feel at your lack of control will transfer to your child as guilt and shame. This is what does the damage, not the incident itself. Victims of assault are encouraged to discuss their experiences, being open about what happened, not endlessly talking in terms of feeling angry towards the people who inflicted the learning, and ideas of revenge. The perpetrators also have their pain and their lessons to learn, possibly more than the victim, depending how far into this role you travel.

Acknowledge that whatever they feel is OK. Their feelings are valid, whatever they are. Look at what they did get right, like not retaliating and giving the bullies an excuse to become more aggressive. Like not allowing the bullies to gain total power over them by giving into any demands. What we usually fail to remember is that bullies are also victims of bullying and their behaviour is usually a reflection of their treatment elsewhere. The bullying child is also a hurting child and the only way they have of feeling any power in their own lives is to exercise it over others as it is exercised over them. If your child is on the receiving end of bullying, don't turn them into a bigger victim, help them to understand the process and, with support, to work it through for themselves.

### Parents who are afraid teach their child to live with fear

Fear is part of being human. It is our warning to care for ourselves. It is essential for our protection but it must not become over protective. Too much fear and we never take a chance in our lives, never explore our potential and self actualise. There are many examples where fear curtails lives. For instance, women who are afraid to go out at night are passing on the message of fear and of 'woman as victim' to both sons and daughters. All emotions attract like to themselves: the more fearful we are, the more likely we are to be attacked either physically or emotionally.

- By using fear to protect your children from attack, what are you teaching them?
- What is more likely to occur later in life?
- When you protect your child, who are you really protecting?
- Which voices are you listening to?
- What lessons are you all learning and what lessons are you avoiding or missing opportunities for?

## The inner voices that guide us

Freud was one of the first people formally to acknowledge the inner voices. He called these the internalised parent and placed them in an area of personality called the **superego**. According to Freud this was not fully developed until around the age of five or six. This is the age at which children are able to make moral judgements of their own. As parents we are all still responding to our own inner voices as well as presenting our child with their own set. These remain in the subconscious unless we change them. If you are truly honest in your answers to the questions above, if your own voices of fear, guilt and shame, that you are lacking as a parent for not protecting your child, are coming through loud and clear, you are over-protecting your own child and passing on to them the same legacy.

The consensus from most parents would be that they would do anything to protect their child and the consensus viewpoint makes us feel that this is therefore the right thing to do. These ideas are challenging and a little confrontational but can you allow yourself to see the value in their argument and let go of your own fear?

## CASE STUDY

### Jane shows self confidence

Jane is a single mother with a young son, Sam. She has a reasonable living and enough money to go out from time to time. She likes to walk rather than drive and walks home alone at night. Sam sees her confident and safe, in control of her life, relaxed and comfortable with her mobility in the community. She is sometimes warned by well meaning friends to be careful but she is confident that nothing will happen to her. She does not take unnecessary risks and is careful, but will not allow her life to be curtailed by fear.

- What message is Jane giving Sam about women? What is he learning?
- What message is she giving Sam about fear?
- What is she continuing to learn from her own experience?

If a woman displays fear of other males, the meta-message that she is giving to her son is that when he is adult, he will be a 'possible risk'. So young boys learn their potential as a source of terror as they are forming their self concept. This will encourage the development of a fear of themselves and their potential, an immediate block to finding love and companionship. Fear, in its many guises, is the emotion which prevents achievement. The meta-messages we give children about other adults contribute to their development of a sense of self.

## WELCOMING THE LESSONS

We have fully learned all that there is to understand about the lesson when we can actually look at the experience and be completely and fully glad that it happened.

If Jane can get to the point in her life where she recognises her association of love and violence, and heal her attraction to power games, she can thank her father, ex-husband and Keith for all they taught her and welcome the experience. She will be able to accept that she needed to go through that experience in order to learn. It is one of the most important positive areas of her life because it was her greatest teacher and will bring her to a freedom that she could not have appreciated properly without that learning.

She can now be discerning and choose not to engage in a similar experience again. You can't appreciate something you've got if you don't know what it is like to be without it. That rule applies to both material and emotional growth. That is the learning which we need to achieve and need to lead our children towards. When Jane and Sam can look back and be glad that he experienced the attack because of the learning which they have both gained from the experience, this will bring them closer rather than setting up a guilt/fear barrier which neither will want and which they will overcome through dependency in order to feel secure, to maintain the sense of closeness.

## CASE STUDY

### Jane learns about anger
Jane was repeatedly patronised and criticised by her mother, Mary. She grew up feeling angry with her mother, unable to believe that Mary loved her. This made her determined to prove her mother wrong and Jane lived with the anger of that rejection for part of her adult life. It wasn't until she had achieved quite a lot in her career, but had been unable to maintain a steady lasting relationship, that she sought counselling. With help she was able to value the lessons that Mary had taught her and heal the anger. She realised that when she stopped being angry with Mary she had learned to become very strong and self reliant. Then she was able to find happiness and be grateful for all her

lessons. It took her 40 years to learn, but the future just got better after that. Mary and Jane finally became friends. Jane hoped that one day Keith would also be able to be a friend.

**SUMMARY**

Parents can identify:

- their own priorities
- their children's priorities
- what and who they are protecting
- how to support the learning of lessons.

# 5
# Disciplining or Devastating Your Child

## UNDERSTANDING DISCIPLINE

Discipline is not something done for its own sake. It has a purpose and is our response to a behaviour from our child. We talk of discipline with a clear intention of what we hope to achieve in our parental role, don't we? Or do we? What exactly do you intend as the outcome of your response, your disciplinary treatment of your child?

My dictionary defines discipline as: 'maintenance of order and obedience amongst pupils, subordinates, etc, corrective punishment, a system of rules and punishments.'

Consider this for a moment:

- What is the outcome you wish to achieve when you discipline your child?

and then answer the following questions:

1. Is the intention similar to the above dictionary definition?
2. Is it intended to prevent them coming to harm?
3. Is it intended to make your life as a parent easier?
4. Is it intended to teach them not to repeat a behaviour/action?
5. Is it intended to teach them to do something differently?
6. Is it intended to help them understand many different ways of doing things, of speaking and acting?
7. Is it intended to enable them to recognise the consequences of their own actions to themselves and to others (without guilt)?

Whatever we as parents think and feel should be examined and questioned in terms of whether we are helping our child in their learning or making it harder for them in the long run in order to make it easier for ourselves in the short term.

## BLOCKING LEARNING

The definition of discipline includes some kind of punishment. Should we even consider using this word in relation to children, especially young children? Yet it is used widely: 'If parents disciplined their children properly, society would have fewer problems'; 'If school teachers still used corporal punishment in school, there would be fewer problems with discipline and disruption in classrooms', etc.

Whenever ideas are presented and accepted as common sense, this is a warning that we are accepting ideas without discernment. Parents should examine these assumptions, and recognise their appeal. As adults we should challenge every assumption we are given and question its meta-message. Throughout history, progress and change occurred because the social rules, values and assumptions were challenged. If we do not challenge and confront rules we do not progress as a society.

By exploring each value and assumption, we can extract whatever we need as parents to teach our children to do the same. Thus children are learning how to choose which rules to adhere to and exactly why they are doing so. Using what parents are getting right already as a basis, and keeping an open mind, we continue to learn and provide our children with a role model for learning which allows them to make successful choices.

### Assessing smacking

There is a great debate about the rights and wrongs of smacking children. Where do you draw lines, when is it reasonable control over your child and when does it become abusive? Children who experience physical assault on their person experience deep fear and humiliation. When is a smack also a physical assault?

*Exercise 5.1 (this is an exercise in empathy)*
- Think of a time when you recently made a mistake or got something wrong, accidentally broke something or otherwise behaved in a way that would not be considered socially acceptable.
- Imagine a giant who is at least twice your size coming into your room, and shouting at you with a very loud voice.
- Now imagine that person hitting you.

Now answer these questions:

- What emotions are you experiencing?
- Do you like this person?
- Do you feel that your action justified this assault?
- What have you learned from this experience?

What was your response to Exercise 5.1? Did you think that you would feel good about the experience? Chances are that you disliked it. Children will feel a range of emotions and need to protect themselves from the fear and humiliation engendered. They commonly use two ways, frequently a confused combination of both:

1. They can be angry with their parents and blame them for the problem, saying that they are wrong. Parents aren't gods and it is all their fault. Children want their parents to be the good guys, to be people that they can be proud of: 'this is my mum/dad'. When we let them down, we let ourselves down too. To compensate for this idea that parents cannot be wrong, the child will then say:
2. Well, I must be wrong, I must be a very bad person if my mum or dad thinks I deserve to be hurt this much.

There are two powerful meta-messages here, so discipline needs to be considered and applied with great care.

**Invading boundaries**

A boundary is a psychological or physical protection which maintains our sense of integrity and wholeness. Boundaries develop with a strong sense of self esteem and personal knowledge. They are flexible and able to discern between relevant and irrelevant assaults on our person, physical or psychological. Boundaries allow us to live our lives successfully and confidently.

Barriers are defence mechanisms which also protect. They are rigid and work from a position of fear. They are very effective in preventing us achieving any goals.

Our body is precious to us and exclusive to us. People who invade that boundary are abusive. It is a form of rape in as much as the damage rape causes is less from the sexual act and more from the violation of the individual and their sense of personal space and integrity. Smacking is an assault on the individual and their boundary, their territory. If people who love us also invade that boundary, either with actual assault in the form of a smack, or with the threat of assault, it is the same thing.

There are two reasons why all smacking and threats are abusive:

1. Abused children are unable to develop boundaries in adult life which allow people to be close to them in a safe way, the basis of any successful relationship. It leads people to learn that abuse and love go together and will either behave like that to a partner or allow behaviour like that towards themselves. It forms part of their unconscious belief system, even if consciously they reject it. The smack itself may last minutes in terms of physical hurt. The actual damage that can be done to a child's self esteem, to their sense of safety and well being, and their right to feel safe and protected, can be very lasting.

2. The more often this kind of discipline is used, the less effective it becomes. The damage is longer lasting, deeper and creates barriers instead of boundaries. This leads to a lack of self discipline.

## AVOIDING SHAME AND GUILT

These two emotions are the biggest cause of under performance and lack of emotional competence.

- We want children to learn lessons.
- We want children to develop healthy boundaries for self protection.
- We must identify relevant lessons:
  - what is the most appropriate approach for enabling a child to learn
  - whilst recognising that there is also a lesson in it for us to learn.

Negative learning experiences through guilt and shame result in a child:

- feeling guilt or embarrassment for being wrong
- being unable to understand the value of getting it wrong

- learning the fear of getting it wrong
- feeling it is they who are wrong rather than something which they have done
- becoming inhibited to all learning for the future.

As the parent you have:

- made your role as parent more difficult for this particular situation
- created a situation where learning will become more difficult
- created resistance to admitting a mistake in the first place so preventing learning occurring
- created resistance to all learning, all change, all personal development within the child.

It is openness to change and the ability to cope with difficulty and ride the ups and downs, the niggles and hassles of life, which personify the emotionally competent individual.

## CONTROLLING OR CARING

Society expects children to be self disciplined and motivated, yet shows little respect for them, little consideration for their needs for safety and room to play, develop and learn, and little consideration for the example we set our children in society. The following points are so obvious and so rarely considered in any depth:

- Why should children respect adults when adults generally do not respect children?
- If we fail to respect children, on what basis can they learn to respect themselves or anyone else?
- How can they experience and learn about respect if they are learning to live without it?

Children learn to distrust the concept of respect, to consider that there must be a hidden agenda, a hidden motive, that nothing can be taken at face value, so why is this person treating me with respect, what do they want?

If we cannot feel respect for ourselves and from others for ourselves, how can we project respect to others? The mirroring principle holds true for society just as much as it does for individuals. The fact that so many children have little respect for others in society is the mirror being shown for society to take a good look at itself.

But as parents we cannot change others, we can only change ourselves. By projecting respect you receive it. The more you respect your child and note their wonderful qualities, the more you will be appreciated, respected and listened to. It is so simple and yet so hard because we as adults need to work on ourselves in order to pass this message on to our children.

## LEARNING STYLES FOR PARENTS

If your children are naughty, that is telling you something about yourself, not about them. Looking inwards is usually the hardest thing to do, but it must be done if we want the best for our child. Focusing on them is transferring the responsibility for us onto them. With that goes all the pressure and burden we are carrying, but doubled for our child. We cannot expect our children to address their behaviour if we do not address our own.

### Applying rules

Parental hypocrisy is a damaging experience for a child. It teaches them to do as others say, not as they do. So which one is right, given that children learn from both instruction and observation? Parents who give a rule and fail to follow it themselves are undermining their own authority. Their child has every moral and reasonable right to challenge that behaviour. If the parent feels threatened and makes this a disciplinary issue, they are compounding the negative experience of the child and obliterating the possibility of positive learning. It is important to make sure that any decisions made are backed up by your own behaviour. What we actually do and what we want to do can differ as long as we recognise this and accept the hypocrisy. If our children are to learn from us they must respect us, faults and all.

### Confusing fear and respect

Many people confuse fear with respect. With due consideration it is easy to see that they are not the same but if we have learned that they go together, they become connected on an internal emotional perceptual level.

Fear:

- prevents us from behaving in certain ways that attract punishment
- teaches how to avoid punishment
- prevents learning and understanding
- does not teach about the behaviour or act as any form of prevention in a real sense because the individual thinks that not getting caught is all that matters
- teaches 'if I can get away with it, then I can do it'.

Children and adults taught through fear are acting without understanding fully why they should not behave in this way. The fear of getting caught can itself become a motivation because it releases adrenaline into our bodies, causing a state of arousal that is exciting and can be addictive. Therefore you are possibly encouraging your child to behave in the opposite way to that which you intend because of the lack of knowledge in the lesson. The real learning is about something quite different.

**Confronting fear**
For young males, confronting fear is a way of testing their bravery and social status as a male. This may explain why crime amongst males is much higher than amongst females and also why female crime rates are rising. They all want to 'feel the fear and do it anyway'. If discipline teaches avoidance of the negative outcome which they can avoid in another way, then they will do so. This is the simple basis for most anti-social behaviour.

If we punish in conventional terms we perpetuate the wrong lesson, the lesson that does not bring an understanding of why they should not want to behave like that for themselves and their own self respect. This is not prevention because if the individual thinks that they can get away without being caught, they will continue. There is no understanding of why they should not behave like this and no self esteem boundaries. This scenario reflects the lack of respect for and from society for many individuals, the mirroring effect mentioned earlier. Discipline should be very much a case of 'do as you would be done by'.

**Approaching discipline**
Positive discipline is helping your child to explore what it was that actually happened; they may well feel bad anyway and do not need it

amplified by your reactions. They may well already feel stupid and unable to believe that they did that. As a parent you have the power to heal and facilitate the learning. Tease out the actual thoughts and feelings by working through a list of questions, all of which avoid the dreaded WHY, which requires the individual to justify their actions and blocks any learning potential. Try this out on yourself first.

*Exercise 5.2*
Think of something that you did which was a mistake and work through the following list of questions:

1. What were your thoughts before doing this action?
2. What did you hope to achieve with this action?
3. What outcome did you achieve?
4. How do the answers to 2 and 3 differ?
5. What could you do differently if the same situation occurs again?
6. What learning has occurred for your benefit?
7. Is there any other way you could have learned such a valuable lesson?

Run through this exercise with your child and summarise the learning. Make them feel good for being honest and open to learning, praise them for their perception. This lengthy and rather tedious process will develop its own shorthand form once you get used to the technique. You can support your child by:

- Helping your child analyse their thoughts and feelings prior and during the offending behaviour; you are enabling them to learn and understand the experience fully.
- Saying that's OK and asking them what they can learn from what has happened. If they feel fear, remove the negative emotion which will block their learning and remind them that we all make mistakes and all learn from experience.

**Using the past constructively**
We cannot undo the past, ever, much as we might like to – it is a waste of energy to think in this negative way. Rather use it

constructively and positively for learning to get it right next time. This positive approach releases the fear immediately because a positive attitude will always override a negative one if you work with it. It allows healing and prevents a build up of guilt, shame and fear which result in poor emotional and physical health in adulthood. Most importantly it facilitates learning – you've learned the lessons.

This is a very different approach to the one assumed as effective in most discussions about disciplining children. It is more demanding on parents to begin with because they have to find their own way through the style and work on their own emotional responses to do with learning and being open to their own mistakes. It is never too late to start this approach and work on it, and don't worry if you get it wrong, be open and discuss this with your child too – you may be surprised at their reaction to your honesty.

The final part of learning and disciplining is to value that mistake. Don't see a mistake – see an opportunity for learning and honour it. See making mistakes as something to be welcomed but not repeated. This requires a very clear boundary of accepting the behaviour and working with it. Any negative connotations will leave a residue of fear in some shape or form and that will require them to hide from the learning in order to escape from the negative feeling.

## Recognising causes of anger

Another important thing to remember with your child is that when we become angry with our children we are more often angry because they have reflected something back to us which we do not like to acknowledge or we fear in ourselves as parents. This makes us feel vulnerable and threatened, often at a subconscious level, but our response to our child is anger, as if they have done something wrong. They will not understand this. So not only are they confused about what they have done wrong but they are then scared of an angry adult who is much bigger and more powerful than them. Is this the way to create respect between you and your child?

Even using jokey threats such as the 'don't make me angry, you won't like me when I'm angry' lines from the Incredible Hulk or other such disguises, you are still being angry and intimidating. (Refer back to Exercise 5.1)

To look at it from a position of empathy, how would you feel if someone at least twice your size came and started shouting at you or even suggested that they might start shouting at you. Would you feel friendly and relaxed, would you be able to listen and communicate easily, would you feel open to learning something about yourself that requires you to admit you made a mistake? And if you had no idea what you have done wrong, would you feel good about the person in front of you or would you feel very insecure and full of fear? Remember that our children are also our teachers and we should respect the lessons they teach us as much as we expect them to respect the lesson we teach them.

So if you feel angry do not look at your child, look at yourself and ask what it is that you do not like to see mirrored back to you. Be honest in the way that you want your child to be, even discuss this with your child. Their clarity and openness often enables them to see the real truth more easily than adults, who hide behind self justifications and complicated explanations. We call this being adult, and understanding the complexities of emotions but it is a clever subterfuge for avoiding being honest with ourselves. For so many people the journey of discovery inside is the most forbidden and fear-filled territory ever, yet it is the key to successful lives. Therefore it is essential for us as parents to make this journey and to share it with our children.

### Knowing you can change

If we project our fear onto our child as anger, we leave them confused and unsure, and they will internalise it, against themselves, because parents can't be that wrong, can they? Oh yes, they can and often are. But they can change too and that is the best part. They can change and they can do it willingly and thoughtfully. If they avoid change their child may see them as imperfect in later life and will invariably have a difficult relationship with both parents and other adults around them in work and personal life. It is not wrong to release your anger, but it is wrong to throw it out at someone else, especially if that person is a child. Being angry is yet another opportunity for you to learn *with* your child by exploring with them, after you have explored yourself, what happened and why it is not their responsibility.

### Putting things right

You have made the mistake of being angry with the child not for something that they have done, but for revealing something that is deep and painful buried within you. You have learned to recognise this and want to heal it. Acknowledge that:

- you have been wrong in the way that you responded
- you are going to learn your lesson from the experience

- it gives you an opportunity to explore what was the root cause of the reaction within yourself
- this is another opportunity for you to learn more about yourself and pass that learning onto your child.

**Learning from your children**

Children of all ages, but especially older than seven or eight, can, in simple terms, understand many of the emotional growth choices that their parents are making. So what better way to improve your child's self esteem than to allow them to be your teacher. They can benefit from that in a positive way: not only do we allow our children to learn their own lessons but we allow them to learn from us by observation rather than instruction. They can see for themselves the benefits to everyone so they also learn to think in this way. If children see that we make mistakes and are human, it has several positive effects:

- They love us anyway and they will love in a whole sense which allows us to be wrong and to be human.
- They will receive a positive meta-message, that it is OK to be wrong, even mum and dad do it.
- By allowing them to openly forgive us and by openly forgiving them we actually heal the incidents as they occur.
- It prevents conflict building into a crescendo and on into adult life.
- It prevents points of conflict continuing within that relationship and filtering through into all adult relationships.

If this approach is adopted, it will become a simple and automatic form of interaction and fit naturally into family relationships. A parent must exercise judgement in terms of explaining why they responded like that, what was the root cause of their response. This is not the same as using your child as unofficial counsellor and absolver. This is a very definite and important boundary.

- Work out your thoughts and feelings using a trained counsellor or trusted friend, away from your child and then go to your child and say 'I am very sorry that I hurt you in this way – it was my problem and not your responsibility'.

- Never try and justify your actions, just state simply that it was a mistake and you are sorry.
- State what you should have done and that you will do that next time.

**Avoiding self justification**

The biggest danger is using your learning and self exploration as a way of justifying your behaviour. This is guilt and avoidance with the double bind of pretending to be honest and open. Nothing justifies it, justification is not needed if we are open to the learning and see where it comes from. We do not need to repeat our mistakes if we have learned from them. We only repeat our mistakes as parents when we are refusing to learn and will continue to do so until we have thought it through fully and learned all there is to know from it. Learning always occurs, whether we fight against it or remain open to it. One way is easier in the end, the open way.

- Be honest and say 'I did this and I was wrong'
- Recognise there is no shame attached to being wrong.
- Do not make excuses for yourself by saying 'I only did this because XYZ'.
- Do not say 'you don't like it when I do it so that's how it feels like when you do it'.

**SUMMARY**

- We all have only one responsibility in life, that is to live as truly to our inner selves as we can.
- As parents our sole responsibility to our children is to love them for their perfection and teach them to be true to themselves.
- We can only do this if we as parents also learn to live like this.
- If we do not, we teach our children to live with the same difficulties as ourselves, the same feelings of guilt, shame, fear and failure.

# 6
# Understanding Love

**DEFINING LOVE**

Although this chapter is quite short, it is a summary of much that has gone before and put into a context of our own and social expectations of the emotional bond between parent and child which we call love. Most people assume that they love their child because he or she *is* their child, and that their child feels the same way about them. Although this is true to a degree, I want to break down the concept of love into several stages. Love is the highest manifestation of joy. Therefore in its purest form **love is the complete absence of fear**.

We use the word love and assume a common understanding and experience. Love is a concept and therefore nothing that we can physically see, hear, measure, touch, taste or smell. We understand it intuitively and this is where the differences come in. A concept as great as love is made up of many smaller ideas which are closely connected. For instance, if I say that 'I love rich chocolate ice cream' does that mean the same as 'I love my children'? Of course not, and no one would really assume that the word in each context actually meant the same thing. In many ways it is more truthful to say 'I love chocolate ice cream' because we are unlikely to experience any fear, whereas we can experience considerable fear attached to our children. The greatest of these is surely fear of loss, which actually causes most parent/child separations at an emotional level. This is a simple example of how varied the ideas are behind the use of this term.

We learn about all the parts of the concept of love from our own experiences. If we experience love in the context of damaging, critical parenting, this is what love feels like for us. This is the same experience of love which has also filled us with low self esteem and self doubt that has held us back in our own development. It is love that is subsumed by fear.

**Analysing love**

Love for both self and another can be broken down to mean the following:

- accepting the other for whatever they are in reality
- recognising the inner core of pure love inside all of us
- respecting their right to make their own mistakes and learn their own lessons
- valuing positive qualities and acceptance of more complex ones
- recognising and valuing the lessons reflected back at us for our own benefit
- accepting that the other is doing the best they can with what they know
- respecting their right to make their own decisions in their own life
- offering supportive feedback when people have learned difficult lessons
- experiencing thoughts and feelings of warmth, concern and interest in the life and well being of the other
- asking for, demanding and expecting nothing
- accepting the present as the only reality and rejecting fear of the past and future.

By now you should have worked through enough of the book to follow this section quite quickly. Simply enough, if you really want your child to grow and learn, give them the space to develop into healthy, emotionally stable and competent adults. This is the meaning of love. The common expectations placed on parents to control and discipline their children are contrary to the development of love and success.

## LETTING GO AND ALLOWING YOUR CHILD TO LEARN

Most parents find that letting go is the hardest aspect of love. Indeed it is hard for all of us. Adults who have experienced broken relationships will recognise particularly just how hard it is and sometimes how long it takes to let go of a relationship which has come to the end of its useful life. But this is what we need to do, and this is almost what we are doing in small stages from the moment a child is born.

We let go physically allowing them to sleep alone as a baby. So the baby learns the lessons of togetherness and separateness on a physical level. Once your child has mastered the skill of balance and can walk, you no longer watch them as carefully. You let them make mistakes – falling over, bumping into things etc, so that they can perfect the technique. This is easy and expected, but the further up the levels we get, the harder it becomes. Letting go allows:

- you to recognise how much your child can achieve without you
- a recognition that you are giving yourself a vote of confidence in your own parenting skills
- you to demonstrate your trust that your own guidance has equipped them to learn their lessons and make sensible decisions
- you to trust and respect them to exercise their learning and discover new lessons.

This is the same level of love that we demonstrate when we support them with their learning. This should be done without recourse to fear, guilt, shame or anger for parent or child. Ask them questions and let them draw their own conclusions, let them find their own learning.

## SUPPORTING YOUR CHILD TO CONFRONT FEAR

Most of the time we are unable to act as we might because we are afraid of outcomes and the responsibility that gives us. It is the burden of responsibility, shored up with fears such as guilt, which turn a simple decision into a major trauma. This may leave us unable to do anything other than remain passive and let things happen to us. This is not the road to success, it is simply a risk-minimising strategy for dealing with life. It is in fact a high risk approach because you may not get the outcome you could have had if you had taken a pro-active role in the decision taking. The only get-out clause is that you didn't overtly do anything, so you can disclaim responsibility. It is important to remember that inactivity is still a decision: a decision not to participate, not to take risks and not to learn. It is common in people who have not been allowed to make risky decisions for themselves in childhood, or for whom the risks that went wrong were heavily laden with negative responses from parents.

Emotional needs require low criticism and high praise for success to grow. Mistakes should not be brushed under the carpet and should not attract criticism. They should be quietly accepted as part of the perfect human being achieving their own perfection through their own lessons.

## When the going gets tough

The hardest times for parents are:

- when children behave in ways which attract disapproval from others, eg family and school teachers
- when children want to extend their sense of freedom and independence before the parent feels ready to let them (but says the child is not ready)
- when children learn some hard lessons, like Sam or Megan
- when children reject something, someone, an interest or viewpoint that is valued by a parent
- when children confront parents with their own worst fears.

The following is a simple exercise which should be useful to adapt to any of the above situations as it arises. Take time to reflect on each of the questions in turn and make a note of your answers:

- What response options do you have?
- What is the most positive outcome of each option?
- How important will the possible best outcome be in five years/six weeks?
- What is the worst that could happen from each option?
- How important will the possible worst outcome be in five years/six weeks?
- How great is the risk of things going badly?
- What is the outcome you want?

This exercise is a mental letting go of fear through rational positive thinking. It releases the tendency to react with fear through either anger or controlling decisions. It allows the parent to discuss their concerns with the child and then allow the child to decide or negotiate and therefore learn to take responsibility for their actions. This will include making mistakes and learning hard lessons but it will result in an adult who is able to make decisions and accept the responsibility for their own lives. It will make them able to act without the restrictions of fear and achieve their potential.

## LETTING GO OF FEAR FOR PARENTS

A child who has learned how to make decisions for themselves within safe boundaries, provided for them by society and family life, is able to participate fully in life as an adult. In order to do this the parent must learn to let go and allow the child to learn his or her lessons. One of the hardest things a parent has to do is to sit back and watch a child making a mistake. The desire to intervene and protect is very great. But as we have seen, protecting children can leave them unable to cope later as adults and undermine their self esteem and independence. If parents hold on to the decision making for children they will feel less fear in the short term. But in the long term they will be unable to trust their child when he or she is out of control/sight. A child who is very restricted at home will usually act in one of three ways when freed from the constraints:

1. They will be unable to make decisions for themselves and not participate in life.
2. They will want to participate in life but be easily led by any influential member of a peer group.
3. They will want to make their own decisions and rush around making them without knowing what they are doing or why.

All these are high risk behaviours for anyone and are common in many young adults and adolescents. It is the result of a society which still talks in terms of controlling children rather than nurturing them. Children who do not have clear personal boundaries, but have developed barriers as a form of self protection, are more likely to desire to conform to a group identity rather than stand alone.

### Thinking for oneself
Research into group conformity clearly showed the importance of knowledge and that confidence in one's own decision is crucial for

withstanding pressure from a group to agree with something against one's better instincts. Crutchfield (1955) showed that people who are more likely to conform with a group, even if they do not believe in the group position, have:

- poorer social relationships
- less leadership ability
- less self sufficiency
- less ego strength
- feelings of inferiority
- a narrow minded and inhibited outlook
- more submissive tendencies
- low self awareness and insight into own emotions.

One of the hardest 'letting go' times in a parent's life is during adolescence, when we have to let them go out in the evenings and often do not know where they will end up. This is when we worry about whether they will take drugs, get into fights, drink and experiment with sex – to list but a few parental nightmares.

If, however, we have allowed our children to make decisions throughout their childhood, they will now use those skills to their best advantage. Group pressure will not lead them into taking undue risks which could have long term consequences. Even if they do start to try out these experiences of adolescence, they will very quickly weigh up the pros and cons and make their own decisions, based on knowledge they have acquired for themselves. Further research (Willis 1963) shows three types of conformity and non-conformity:

1. Those who move towards the majority group norms and adhere to them.
2. Those who move toward anti-majority group norms and oppose the majority but still adhere to a minority group norm.
3. Those who have a lack of consistency in moving toward or away from a group norm and remain independent of the group generally.

Children are not born into one of these groups, they are socialised into them. Only people in group 3 are free from the group rule and are therefore more likely to make their own decisions and stick to them. These are the people who have learned their lessons and are comfortable with themselves. These are successful people.

## TRUSTING YOUR CHILD

So you have finally allowed yourself to sit back and let go. Your child is now making their own decisions and learning the skills that will enable them to mature into balanced adults. You are letting them make their own mistakes and showing confidence in their ability to make decisions and accept responsibility for the consequences of their actions. They will still make mistakes and those mistakes may have quite serious consequences, but they are still young and will learn fast at this stage if they are allowed to. This is the greatest sign of respect that you can give your child. The meta-message of trust and respect for their judgement and ability to deal with errors of judgement will have several effects:

- They will be comfortable with their achievements.
- They will remain open to learning from their mistakes.
- Their self esteem and self confidence will continue to grow.
- They will become more self reliant.

## SUMMARY

- Love is the absence of fear.
- Trusting yourself and your child to learn and grow from life experiences is the greatest way of demonstrating love.
- Recognise that the individual who can make their own judgements and decisions and accept responsibility, can only do this through their sense of acceptance of all that they do, think, feel and say.

# 7
# Using Stories as Metaphors

The tradition of story-telling travels throughout history and lives within all cultures. Scheherezade kept herself alive by telling stories that were sufficiently compelling to keep her audience and would-be executioner interested. Within Arab culture story-telling was recognised as a way to earn a living – the better you were at telling your stories to the audience in the market, the more successful. Other cultures set aside special times, such as marriage or transitional life stages, for telling stories and have stories for specific times of the year, such as after the harvest. Story-telling has a long tradition of oral performance. The stories were seen as rich treasure which would be passed on, as well as the correct way to tell them; as each story-teller developed their own interpretation, the stories have evolved over time.

In our culture it is very much the tradition to share stories with young children at bedtime, usually in order to calm a child and give them something imaginative and fun to think about before they sleep. The choice of story is quite important, as anything which arouses strong emotions will have an opposite effect to helping the child sleep.

Story-telling is a tradition in nursery and primary schools. Because this is during the day, it is possible to use material which is more challenging. Some children enjoy stories which contain quite extreme violence. The safety of a fictional setting allows exploration of these feelings without actually putting anyone at risk.

## DEVELOPING IMAGINATION

The imagination is both a versatile tool and a rich resource for humans to work with. From the imagination comes all creative and original thought. Without it we would never have evolved as a species. Yet this incredible gift that we have is dismissed as 'just your imagination', ie not real. How real is a thought? It is a thought that initiates all advance, all inventions, all progress, all learning and knowledge, all scientific and medical progress. Thought creates

# Using Stories as Metaphors

reality in a material sense just as much as in a perceptual sense. Our thinking patterns are the richest source we have and the most innovative thoughts come from the imagination. Imagination works from the unconscious mind and the right side, creative brain.

By using stories, imagery and metaphor, it is possible to access the learning patterns laid down within the banks of previous experience. It is possible to develop new ones for specific purposes. Most learning is held subconsciously and we remain unaware of how and why we feel certain things. Yet these experiences affect our immediate behaviour and the perception of new experiences.

Stories work with both the conscious and unconscious mind. We relate on both levels, are stimulated on both levels, conjure up a visual representation from the words, relate to the emotions and behaviour of characters within the stories. And stories are a rich resource for art, with many representations from stories like St George and the Dragon, Venus and Mars, Adam and Eve, the Trojan Horse, to name but a few.

In order to maximise this connection and enhance the learning from each story, there are a range of practical activities you can carry out with your child. Select one that will interest your child the most and maximise their abilities rather than choosing one that you might think most suitable. These stories must be explored by the child in the way that is most attractive for them if any incidental learning is to occur.

## Activities
1. Draw themselves in a similar way to one of the characters in one of the stories.
2. Draw pictures to go with each story; model characters from clay, collage, wall frieze.
3. Turn one of the stories into a carton picture strip with speech balloons.
4. Write a poem based on one of the stories.
5. Write a speech from one of the characters explaining how they felt about what happened.
6. Write a story of themselves in a way that is similar to one of the stories, eg the holly tree; think about a time when they felt different, outside, unnoticed, alone, with low self esteem.
7. Rewrite the story with a different ending.
8. Rewrite the story from the point of view of a different character, eg the fox, or Violet's parents.
9. Make a list of things that they like about themselves. Really

help them to develop this list.
10. Make a list about all the things that they don't like about themselves. Really help them to develop this list as well.
11. Discuss each of the items on this list and discuss ways of showing that these things might also be good in a different situation.

## USING EMPATHY

If we enjoy a story we will have become involved, we will have thought, felt and allowed the story to become part of us, our whole experience, for the amount of time it has taken to listen. Like emotions, stories have energy but they also hold symbolism, which is why they are healers. This energy is like electricity in many ways, a story can enlighten you, animate you, motivate you, extend you and offer you endless possibilities but you cannot see it, only the result of it.

### Choosing the right time

Stories which are told at the wrong time and in the wrong way can have little or no desired effect at all. Coercing a child to listen to a story will hold little benefit. It is willingness and enjoyment which enhances the learning and enables a child to be relaxed and open to the learning contained within the story. Children who have had very difficult lives are encouraged by therapists and care workers to make stories of their own lives as a way of finding their own identity and healing.

Stories allow us as parents to discuss difficult and sometimes painful issues with our child from a safe distance. It is the position of security which allows us to remain confident and open to the learning. Making a child feel fear in advance of a situation will make it harder for them to cope if the reality occurs, and will make it more likely to occur.

- How else can you prepare a child for the possibility of bullying at school or help them cope with domestic violence?

- How can a child explain their lack of confidence or self esteem before they understand the concepts behind it and the language to use?

Life will never be perfect and indeed I hope that this book has demonstrated the importance of facing and dealing with difficulty as essential to emotional development. There will always be other people who are hurt or damaged in their experience of life and these are the people we have to learn to cope with. They have to learn to cope with their own lives and the only responsibility anyone has is to themselves and to their children, to teach them how to be responsible for themselves.

The stories at the end of this book are designed to be flexible in the range of issues they explore. By talking about the experiences of a fictional character, a child is able to identify their thoughts and feelings through empathy with the experiences of the character in the story. This is a basis for story-telling throughout history and across cultures. It is the basis of the excellent book by Estes called *Women Who Run With Wolves*, which looks at all the original folk stories and the commonality of themes across cultures. I have adapted a fable by Aesop, extended it, and written two original stories in addition.

Using the child's natural empathy with the characters in the book a parent can prepare and discuss issues that have already arisen or might arise. Certainly the more prepared a child is before an event the more ably they will cope with it and not be taken by surprise. Sharing stories with our child can be the safest situation from which to learn about life's nasty surprises. It is the security and intimacy of this setting which allows informal and very effective learning to take place. It is possible to discuss the issues in a story as it is followed through, stopping and discussing aspects, or reading the story through and then using it as a basis for discussion of life experiences.

## ACCESSING THE UNCONSCIOUS MIND

The unconscious mind is easily accessed through the right brain because it does not engage the logical conscious left brain thought processes. In dreams we are presented with a range of stories in which we are involved and often so are those around us from everyday life. The contents of dreams are often recalled as disjointed and quite impossible in our conscious sense of reality but in the dream it happened. Up until a century or so ago people would dream of flying and think it quite ridiculous, yet flying is now seen as a normal method of travel.

### What is dreaming?
Much work has been done on the importance of dreaming, how long it lasts and how often it occurs. It is usually reckoned to occur during REM (rapid eye movement) sleep (Dement and Kleitman) and there is evidence that some people experience lucid dreaming, ie dreams that the dreamer is controlling (Hearne). But we are still

unsure why we dream. Jung and Freud both believed that dreams are the best and most accurate access to understanding the unconscious mind. Dreams are seen as a way of working out emotional conflicts and living fantasies in safety.

Stories allow us to think about experiences from a different perspective. We can reframe the experiences of a child from negative to positive by using a story which shows how outcomes can be unexpected and difficulties often turn out to be the best thing that could have happened. The child might be part way through a difficult time in their lives, or still experiencing the difficulty even if it has ended in actuality, but because of the negative emotions connected to the experience, they are blocked from gaining any benefit. Stories can be used to extend and open up these possible futures for a child and help them to see that all is not lost. Good things come round too and if we are too busy feeling sorry for ourselves we might just miss the opportunity.

Many experiences can be too painful for us to cope with at a conscious level and in a direct way, but stories can penetrate the defence mechanisms in a safe and indirect way, thus allowing changes to occur. This is a powerful form of emotional healing that is used by therapists and in many forms. It is also the basis of other art therapies. Jung believed that creativity is essential for mental health.

Stories are healing because we become disconnected from ourselves for a short period of time and for the duration of the story we can forget our own limitations and become anything we choose, identifying with characters in the story. Children often like toys which they associate with stories from books or TV characters, and will play games which extend this fantasy of endless possibilities in a completely safe way. In the same way many adults like to read escapist books and see high adventure, fast action films in a way that is safe.

**Getting the most out of stories**
The more you put yourself into the story the more medicine you receive, the more learning, the more healing and the more understanding you get. It is very much a question of what you give out, you get back. There are no mistakes in life, only lessons to be learned. The more prepared for the exam we are the better. Real experience is the exam, stories are the swotting. The more swotting we do, the better the outcome. Let us not slip into the idea that we can wing it on the day – maybe we will and maybe we won't but it will be much harder that way. Swotting for life using stories is really not as hard as swotting for school exams and if you and your child share the experience, the learning will be wonderful.

The language of stories and poems is very often similar to the experiences we have in dreams, but in a more cohesive form. A story can go anywhere and take any form. It is not real but it can represent real life and it can feel real. Dream analysis has been understood for centuries and across healing perspectives as central to understanding the mind and the influence of mind over body. Dreams occur in an unconscious state and the interpretation is done at a conscious level. Stories are experienced at a conscious level and penetrate the subconscious.

## TEACHING THROUGHOUT HISTORY

Story-telling as a means of teaching about life has many very significant models of excellence. All the major religions use stories to illustrate a point. The Bible is a rich source of stories which can be told for their own interest, and which enable us to consider ideas and situations in a non-religious way if we choose. All the great philosophers used stories as a way of explaining the growth and development of the individual through adversity. Many of the myths of Greece, Rome, Egypt and other ancient cultures are evidence of this. Think back to stories you read as a child:

- How did they affect you and influence you?
- Were they treated as stories and therefore not to be taken seriously?
- How many of them do you still remember in a special way?

Unfortunately too often western society dismisses creative thought as not being logical and yet it is only creative thought which brings about changes and sees alternative solutions to problems. It is through creative thought that we really can explore the full creativity of our humanity.

### Reviving the story-telling tradition

Historically stories were used to teach about life, but in modern western culture there seems to be too much emphasis on using stories as 'an enjoyable way of learning to read'. In other words the story is only a means of acquiring one skill needed in adult life and this is its primary function. It is not seen as a special and useful tool in its own right and this deprives many children and adults of the real value of stories which is to learn about life in safety. The tradition of the spoken story is mostly lost. Very few people go out for an evening to listen to someone telling stories, yet this often happened in inns and on street corners in previous centuries. Performance poetry is still a minority interest which is supported mainly by other poets. Cheaper publishing techniques have made books more accessible. Films and TV are other ways of experiencing stories, but none is as rewarding as having a story read to you. The nearest we get to that is in childhood while we are learning to read and the pleasure of reading can be destroyed as part of this process. Children with dyslexia find it hard to read for themselves, but because they often have better visual imagery skills, they can memorise the story from hearing it and enjoy a far richer and more imaginative interpretation of the story content.

Stories are like gifts from the teller to the listener. It is a giving of your time and all your concentration in the telling of the story. It is a gift of your skills in using different tone and volume, in giving voices to the characters in the story, of placing emphasis and emotion into the story. This has valuable meta-messages for a child. It is telling them that they are worth your effort.

**Reading a story well**

It is always a good idea to prepare yourself for reading a story by knowing it in advance. Then you can concentrate on using your voice to bring it to life. There is a significant difference in hearing a story read by someone who has read it through a couple of times and has prepared themselves to become involved with the telling.

The stories at the end of this book have a breakdown of suggested interpretations and follow-up activities. If you read the stories first before you talk to your children you can read the breakdowns of each story so that you can explore the issues more fully. You can also find a greater range of possible uses for each story. You may find that you will also see the stories in a newer and deeper light. You may find yourself thinking and learning from them yourself. Stories are not just for children. Adults can gain as much from a child's story and even more since they will identify the ironies and subtleties more clearly.

Stories that are written as metaphors can be revisited because they mean something different each time. Life will have continued throwing you opportunities for learning and your perception will continue to grow. The story of the fox and the blue grapes might mean bullying one week and feeling insecure and unable to communicate the next.

Children can rewrite the story in their own words. This is a good way of discovering how they have interpreted the story and what they have identified within it. Follow-up activities extend the depth to which the child has empathised with both the characters and the experiences in the story.

# The Stories

# The Little Holly Tree

A long time ago, deep in the middle of a very old forest, there grew a young holly tree. She grew tall and strong, growing up towards the sky, until she was nearly as big as some of the other trees around. For many years the holly tree put so much energy into growing that she didn't notice all the other trees in the forest.

Then one day the little holly tree stretched out her long branches, shook her prickly dark green leaves and looked around. Standing right next to the holly tree was a tall chestnut tree. His branches and twigs were covered with buds but they were all sticky and brown. 'How strange', thought the holly tree, looking at her own tiny green ones. 'I wonder why the chestnut tree is so different', thought the little holly tree. Then the holly tree shook her branches and rustled her leaves a little more to wake up the sleepy old chestnut tree, but he stood dozing in the spring sunshine.

Suddenly the forest started to fill with lots of different noises. Squeaks and shouts and stomps and thumps. The holly tree didn't know what these noises meant so she looked around eagerly to see what was happening. She felt quite excited at all the new things that she was seeing for the first time.

At that moment lots of children came running through the trees. They came running up to the chestnut tree and danced around him, all holding hands and singing and calling out to each other. Then they stopped dancing and started to pick some of the twigs with the big brown buds on. As they did so the holly tree could hear them talking. 'How nice the twigs will look when the leaves start to open. We can put them in pots of water and stand them on the window sills.'

The holly tree was fascinated and waited for the children to turn around and take some of her buds home too. She rustled her leaves proudly and shook her branches, but the children didn't take any of the holly tree's twigs at all. None of the children seemed even to notice the holly tree, no matter how hard she tried to shake her branches and rustle her leaves. When the children had gone, she stopped looking around for a few days. The forest suddenly seemed too quiet and lonely. But she was too curious to know about everything and she soon started to look around again.

Nearby was a hawthorn tree close to the edge of the wood. The hawthorn tree was looking very dainty, covered in snowy white blossom and fresh light green leaves with pretty edges. 'How pretty you are', thought the holly tree, looking at its own plain green leaves with sharp prickles all around the edges. She looked at her flowers too, but they were so small that you could hardly tell they were there. And she felt a little sad.

Then the holly tree heard the noises of singing and dancing and cheered up very quickly. 'Maybe the children have come to see me this time,' she thought. The children came running and dancing into the forest. They were carrying all sorts of bags and blankets. They ran right past the holly tree and up to the hawthorn tree. They joined hands and danced around her, just as they had around the chestnut tree. The little holly tree looked on, still hoping that they would visit her this time. But the children stopped their dances and collected some of the may blossom. They clipped it into their hair and danced around the hawthorn tree all over again, laughing and clapping with joy. Then the oldest children took out a big rug and spread it out under the boughs of the hawthorn tree. They all sat down on it to eat their picnic.

The holly tree watched the children and thought how nice it would be if they came to dance round her when they had finished eating. But when they had finished their picnic, they all danced round the hawthorn tree once more, then went home. The holly tree didn't like her dark prickly leaves any more. She wanted soft light green leaves like the other trees and big white blossoms. She drooped her branches a little and decided not to look around so much.

A few weeks later the holly tree heard the sound of the children coming back into the forest again. She didn't look up to begin with. But soon her curiosity got the better of her and she wondered if they might come and see her this time. Still the children didn't come near to the holly tree. This time they went to the old beech tree that stood in the centre of the forest. His big branches were low to the ground and spread out wide across the forest. The children climbed into the beech tree. Some climbed up a little way and some climbed right up to the top of the tree. They used the patterns of sunlight on the branches to make their games. They played games of pirate ships and tree houses and all sorts of adventures. The older children just climbed up and up, to show how high and how brave they were.

The little holly tree looked at the smooth strong branches of the beech tree and then she looked at all the slim branches of her own, that grew so close together they did not allow the sunlight through. She knew that the children could not ever play with her like that. She hung her branches even lower and tried not to mind about the children ignoring her. But she felt so lonely and so ugly.

As the shadows grew longer the children packed up their games and went home. They were all laughing and talking to each other as they walked through the forest. The holly tree watched them disappearing and felt sad all over again. It looked such fun having all those children climbing and playing their games with you. Maybe she should try and grow a bit more and see if they would come and play with her then. But no matter how hard she tried she could not grow any faster.

A few weeks later still, the children came back into the forest. This time they carried bags and sticks and sacks. They stood around the great oak trees that grew next to each other over in the far corner of the forest. They threw the sticks up into the branches of the great oak trees and started to collect the acorns that fell down. They were talking about how they would feed them to the pigs that lived in the farmer's field in the village. The big old black and white sow would come and rub her back along the fence when the children fed her the acorns. When they had filled all their boxes and sacks, they packed everything up and went back to their homes.

The holly tree looked at her tiny hard green berries. You could hardly see them, hidden in between the hard prickly dark green leaves. She wondered how she could get the children to come and play with her but, try as she might, she could only grow dark green prickly leaves and lots of thin branches that grew too close together.

Then the wind began to grow a little harder and a little colder. The sun didn't come and shine her warm smile into the forest so much. The leaves on all the other trees began to change into the most beautiful colours you could imagine. The forest looked as if someone had thrown pots of paint all over it. There were reds and yellows and browns and oranges and even some colours that looked like purple. Now the children came and danced through the piles of leaves that had been swept up in corners by the wind. They collected all the sticks and twigs that had been thrown down by the trees and made a small fire surrounded by big stones. They were very careful to make sure that the fire could not hurt the forest. And they all danced and roasted chestnuts from the sweet chestnut tree that grew in another corner of the forest.

None of the children came near to the little holly tree. They did not collect her twigs and leaves because they were too sharp and prickly to touch. Now she really hated her leaves and branches. She longed to be like the other trees in the forest and make the children want to come and play with her. But nothing was going to change the shape of her leaves or the size of her branches. She could only ever be a holly tree because that was what she was.

The little holly tree felt so sad and lonely that she did not notice the wind getting colder and colder. She did not notice the small white flecks that started to come with the wind. She did not notice how bare all the other trees looked with their leaves all fallen and blown around in the mud. She only thought of how many times the children came into the forest and did not come to visit her.

One day, when she was feeling very sad and sorry indeed, she heard the children come back into the forest. This time she did not look to see where they were going to play. She closed her ears and eyes tight so that she did not know they were there. She did not see them walking towards her. She did not hear them saying 'What beautiful red berries the holly tree has now, and look how dark and green she stands, against all the other trees with no leaves any more.'

Then the children began to dance around the little holly tree. They sang songs about how beautiful her berries were. How she would give food and shelter to all the birds through the winter hiding underneath her thick dark leaves and slim tangled branches. They danced and circled her until she started to look up and smile. Then she rustled her leaves and shook her berries a little more. The children had come to see her. They were singing about her and dancing round her in circles. Then they thanked the holly tree for giving them some of her leaves and berries to put in their homes to brighten the winter. The holly tree felt so proud that now she was the only tree in all the forest that the children came to and she gladly gave them some of her leaves and berries to take home.

The next spring, when the children came to visit the chestnut trees, she enjoyed watching their games. She smiled to herself and thought, 'it will be my turn again soon enough', and she never felt sad again.

# Thinking about 'The Little Holly Tree'

There is the potential, in all three stories, for several interpretations of meaning and applications. First of all write a list of your own impressions and thoughts on this story. Does your list include the following areas:

- loneliness
- wanting to be special
- feeling different
- starting a new stage in life
- being impatient
- being confused
- experiencing prejudice
- starting a new school
- making new friends
- reaching puberty?

Compare your list with this one and see how similar your ideas are. Write a brief summary of one of your own experiences which fits in with one theme from this story.

- Does this exercise make any difference to your understanding of that experience?
- What are the differences?

Hopefully, if there are any differences, it is because, using the story, you have learned a little more from that experience, even if it happened many years ago. The learning never stops because it is always possible to see things from a new perspective.

### Identifying the themes
The following breakdown of possible interpretations can be worked through in any order relevant to you and your child's life. Many of

the themes overlap, just as real life experiences overlap each other. Please read them and adapt them to your own and your child's experiences.

**Loneliness**
The holly tree looks around and sees all the other trees in the forest. She tries to communicate with them but they do not want to reply. We can all feel like this at times, when we are surrounded by people and lots of things are happening but somehow we are not being heard.

Children can feel like this very easily in a family that is busy and full of activity, focusing on certain priorities that are seen as the most important in the family welfare. But somewhere deep inside the family one person is not being heard. And they feel lonely. They may try everything to get attention and after repeated failure they gradually withdraw. The holly tree ruffled her leaves and shook her branches but she learned that she could not to get the attention she wanted and she gradually loses interest in what else is happening in the forest. Why should she be interested in any one else if they are not interested in her?

Eventually the children do come and dance around her and she glows with pride. In many ways this is too easy and the story suggests that one simple gesture will put it all right. But our holly tree is very wise because she is a tree. Children need more explanation and understanding to enable them to heal quickly. Children do have a similar kind of wisdom to the holly tree, they do not get caught up in endless hypothetical justifications for things, they see things in very simple terms and the holly tree's simplicity is representing the child in this way. This story can help a child to understand that they do not need to feel lonely but it can also be used to help a child explain how they feel.

**Wanting to be special**
Another use for this story could be that the children represent family, parents, and the holly tree is a child trying to get attention. It feels very lonely and her self esteem is dropping all the time as she is more and more ignored. This teaches us as parents to give regular and consistent attention to our children, but not to focus on them all the time. Otherwise they become nothing more than performing seals in the family. However cute they are, do not fall into the trap of over attention.

However, being aware of your child and all the progress it makes in life, right from the beginning, is important. Or, like the holly tree, their sense of self will be diminished and result in a loss of self worth and self esteem. This is a problem because then they will do almost anything to attract attention and this is where the risks come in. A naughty child is usually trying to attract attention and any attention is better than nothing.

So like a child starting anything new, the holly tree is very optimistic and enthusiastic and wants someone to notice her in the same way that she has started to notice those around her. She doesn't have a very strong sense of self yet, and is looking for a response from the other trees and the children, to see how she fits in. Her enthusiasm reminds me of young children who have not been thwarted in their development and some adults who still retain this fresh enthusiasm for new projects, ideas and adventures into old age. But equally a teenager can begin to experiment with identities and a developing sense of independence and adventure in their life. Both of these stages are essential for their development into adulthood.

**Feeling different**
Many children feel different at some stage of their life for a number of reasons. Many of these reasons are covered elsewhere in this analysis. The point of this story is that it illustrates the differences that exist but it also shows that there is nothing wrong with them. The holly tree really dislikes herself because she feels different, and she does not see the value of her differences for a long time.

We are all dependent on other people to reflect our value back to us and the feedback information is an essential part of our growing awareness of self, of who we are. The holly tree eventually learns that she too, like everyone, has value in our own way. It just takes her some time to be able to recognise her own special value, and she is only able to do that through being recognised and rewarded by the children dancing around her and telling her how lovely she looks. Most of us have characteristics which have their advantages and disadvantages. The holly trees sees her dark evergreen leaves only as a disadvantage until the advantage is clearly shown to her. Most of the time we concentrate on looking at the disadvantages of our personalities and do not spend enough time thinking about the advantages.

## UNDERSTAND THE DEVELOPMENTAL STAGES OF CHILDHOOD

### Early childhood

Initially in the story the little holly tree is suddenly awakened and looking around, getting to know her environment. In many ways she represents the *tabula rasa* model of the child, a blank sheet on which life will write her story. She does not know what to expect and is full of hopeful and joyful expectation. Although most people do not really see the child as a blank sheet, we all do acknowledge that the child is ready to learn everything it will need to survive. It is programmed to do so and most significant learning will have already taken place by the age of five. This early stage is usually the template for future experience and interpretation. It establishes a sense of 'normal'.

### Mid childhood

The holly tree was born some time ago but has gone through a higher transformation of consciousness. These types of transformation occur in children's lives in several ways. It is the fine tuning of experience and success in the social world that takes place. There is a distinct change in the way a child views friends and friendship, moral dilemmas and many other aspects of their life at this age.

They begin to see other people as more than just available for their convenience and deep and lasting friendships can begin at the age of about seven years old. Several developmental psychologists such as Piaget and Bruner have noted that children of this age experience a change in the level of awareness of those around them. Donaldson and Hughes saw it as the ability to think from the perspective of another, what Piaget called to 'decentre'.

This transition does not happen in one go, it has been occurring as a gradual process for several years but this is seen as a watershed in emotional development because it represents the ability to take responsibility. In other cultures this is the age when girls are expected to take care of the younger siblings while the mother deals with the new babies and other household duties. A boy is expected to take responsibility for a small group of cattle or donkeys or contribute to the work of the men.

In modern society these rites of passage are denied to our children and there is very little marking this transition. Yet it should not be forgotten. This is the time when your child can really start to use stories to learn from because they could imagine themselves in the shoes of the character in the story. This represents a child's growing awareness of their experiential field and their place in it, and especially their ability to empathise.

**Being adolescent**
This is a stage where the child has to develop yet another sense of identity for themselves. They have to participate on a more equal level with adults and that can seem scary. Rather than being the little tree growing up, the holly tree is now big enough to compare herself with the other trees around her.

The new sense of identity in adolescence is not just about physical changes but more to do with all the social and emotional changes which accompany it. Now she wants to participate in the activities in the forest but she doesn't really know how. To begin with all her attempts fail and she feels dejected and a failure. She withdraws rather than risk any more failure.

In adolescence many of the challenges feel like climbing Mount Everest and represent a major challenge for the young adult. They need support and encouragement to continue, just as the holly tree receives the support and interest from the children and then is able to understand her place in the seasons of the forest, so the young adult will need to learn that they must find their own place. They must learn that it will not be offered to them as soon as they open their eyes to look for it.

**Being impatient**
Many children are very impatient and want to make things happen immediately. Yet as Daniel Goleman suggests, waiting for the longer term reward is often more satisfying and shows a level of maturity and restraint which is a sign of potential success in adult life. Accepting that everything has its time and its season is important and the holly tree has to wait for the full cycle of seasons from spring right through to winter in order to find out what her reward is. She finds it hard to wait and gives up hope, yielding to feelings of low self esteem and hopelessness. But recognising that the goodies do arrive if you wait for them gives her a new and more mature perspective on life and she is then able to recognise the value and pleasure of waiting and anticipation.

**Being confused**
In this story the holly tree has certain expectations of how she will be received and when they are not fulfilled she is confused and hurt.

She feels somehow that she is in the wrong place and nothing about her experiences seems to be good. In fact nothing about her self seems to be good. Children sometimes experience this in a number of ways and at different times in their lives, usually connected with other changes in life which are addressed elsewhere in this analysis.

**Experiencing prejudice**
This story could be a discussion of racism or disability and shows that even if one person seems to be different in a very obvious way, we are all different. The story shows how all the trees are different in many ways, but they are all trees. Therefore those differences should be valued and of course are valued by enlightened people who teach acceptance of all others whatever they have done or appear to be. It is our very humanity which makes us more similar than any minor detail of difference. The holly tree is still a tree even if she doesn't lose her leaves in winter like all the other trees. But, like children who are the brunt of unkindness and ignorance from others, she begins to hate her leaves and her flowers and her branches and everything that makes her herself. She sees only the disadvantages in them all compared with the other trees.

This loss of self esteem is experienced by children on so many levels and in so many ways that the parent could apply it to any experiences that the child may have had. It's not until much later in the year that she begins to understand the value of her differences and learns to understand their contribution to the children who come to the forest, thus keeping the continuity of their relationship with the forest going even through the winter. She is the one they choose to turn to when the weather becomes too cold to spend much time in the forest any more. She is their reminder of their love of the forest and all the good things in life that await the new spring. Thus the cycles of life and living are experienced through the seasons of the forest.

**Starting a new school**
This can feel very intimidating, especially if it is a new area and there will not be anyone to go with on the first day. Of course most sensitive teachers will select a child to take care of the new one until they find their own way, but sometimes this is not enough. This story could be used to help a child understand and interpret their fears about such changes. The important thing is to not make the child feel silly for being unsure of the unknown but to help them to see that the unknown is a new opportunity for learning and

exploring. What we learn from the holly tree is that to begin with no one really is interested in her. The other children (trees) have been around for longer. They know who's who and what's what and they don't need to take her into account. So she feels increasingly lonely. This may only be for the first week for the child but a week can seem like an awfully long time when you are going through change. As the holly tree's year progresses, she starts to retreat more and more and loses her self esteem and her enthusiasm. Her confidence and interest has not been responded to by those around. Then she is surprised when suddenly the children come and visit her and choose her to dance around. This teaches the child that they cannot expect to be the centre of attention and they have to wait to find their niche in the new situation.

So the holly tree learns to be patient and wait her turn. She learns that she does not have to be the centre of the attention all the time but that everyone should have their turn. She learns that by waiting she will have her time of recognition and that each of the trees has their special quality. This may not always be obvious, but at the right time it is clear how each tree provides the forest with all that it needs, and also the children who visit it.

### Reaching puberty

The transformation of the holly tree is also a representation of moving from one stage to another in life, and one of the most significant transformations is puberty. Because we still live in a society where sex is largely an under discussed issue other than in terms of censorship or exploitation, it is therefore a potential emotional minefield for our children in terms of their changing sense of self.

It also shows the importance of not conforming with everyone else. It is the essential differences in all of us that are the richness and our resources. We need all of those differences. The holly tree's thick sharp leaves could be seen as a disability that a child has, but like all of us, what we don't have in one area we make up for in another. Some of the most disabled children are also the greatest sources of spontaneous affection and *joie de vivre*. Their differences are a lesson to us all.

### SUMMARY

Almost as soon as a child opens their eyes, they begin to learn about their family and environment so that they can survive and become part of it. There is much argument within psychology about whether the urge to learn and grow is biologically or environmentally stimulated, but in many ways it is more important to know that it happens to every child and is part of their development. As I have said before, it is essential not to protect your child from experiences, but there are key stages in a child's life which present challenges. These challenges are the best opportunities for parents to teach their children to understand and become more emotionally competent.

**Questions to ask your child for discussion**
1. What would have happened if the holly tree had got **all** the attention every time the children came into the forest?

2. What did she have to learn?

3. Was it easy for her to learn this lesson?

4. Could she have learned this lesson any other way?

5. What could the other trees in the forest have done to help her?

# The Fox and the Blue Grapes

Long ago, deep in the forest, there grew a vine. She was a most unusual vine and grew the most unusual blue grapes. She loved the days in the sunshine in her little corner of the forest and spoke to the trees around her. They were her friends. They loved to laugh together and rustle their leaves.

Many animals would come to taste the sweet blue grapes of the vine. Squirrels came to play in her branches and tickle her with their tiny little claws. Birds would come and sing to her. The wind would come and flutter her leaves and share his thoughts with her. She loved them all.

One day a fox was walking through the forest. The vine saw the fox. His sleek red coat and long bushy tail glinted in the sunlight. She saw how handsome he was. He played games and did tricks for her. He started to visit the vine often. The vine would look forward to his arrival.

She loved to watch him play, rolling around on the ground. He would roll over and over, as if he would never stop. It made her laugh. She watched eagerly each day to see what games he would invent next. He made her laugh even more than the squirrels did with their tiny claws. Even more than the wind did with the stories of his travels. Even more than the birds did with their funny little songs.

The vine grew to love the fox and gave him big bunches of her beautiful blue grapes. These were the sweetest grapes that the fox had ever tasted in his life and he began to long for the grapes. He wanted them, more and more. If he went off into the forest, he would always hurry back and play under the vine and she would give him her fruit to show how much she loved him. And when he lay down to rest after playing his games for her, she would stroke his fur with her tendrils and soothe him to sleep under her branches.

Soon the fox started to feel worried that someone else might want to take the grapes from the vine. He didn't want her to share her grapes with the squirrels and the birds any more. He wanted the vine all for himself.

The thought inside his head grew and grew until he could not bear the idea of anyone else wanting *his* blue grapes, because that is what he now thought. He forgot that the grapes were a gift from the vine. He forgot that the vine gave them to him in return for the games that made her laugh. These thoughts made him very scared. And very angry. The more he thought these thoughts, the more scared and angry he became. He still came to the vine every day but he did not play so much. Still the vine gave him her beautiful big blue grapes, as much as he could eat.

One day the fox came to the vine and said nothing at all. He did not play or try to make the vine laugh. He tried to chase away the birds that sang high in her branches. He could not reach them and they laughed at him. This made the fox very angry indeed. He threw stones at them to make them fly away. Then he snatched at some grapes hanging down above his head. He took all that he wanted. He forgot to thank the vine.

The vine watched sadly. She missed the singing of the birds in her branches. When the fox had eaten all the grapes that he could manage, and was very full, too full to move, he lay down. The vine wanted to stroke his fur to make him feel happy again. He was too angry and moved away. The vine couldn't reach him.

As he slept, the fox felt cold and unhappy. He had many bad dreams. He missed the soft tendrils stroking his fur as he slept. He became more and more angry with the vine because she did not stroke his fur any more. He forgot that she could not move her feet like he could. He forgot that it was he who had gone to sleep too far away for her to reach him.

Then the fox had an idea. He would show everyone that the vine was his and belonged to him.

As he stuck the knife into the bark of the vine she cried out and begged him to stop. She tried to stroke him and to offer him grapes but he ignored her. He was determined to make sure that no one else would get his vine and that no one else would want her. The vine could feel her sap dripping from the cuts that he made with the knife. She thought that she would die.

When the fox had finished he smiled to himself. His name now showed proudly on the bark of the vine. He could hear the sadness of the vine but he ignored her. She was his vine now. He lay down and went to sleep, close to the vine. He waited for the vine to stroke him but she did not. She was busy making new bark to cover up the cuts that he had made and to stop her sap from dripping away. She kept her tendrils to herself.

When the fox woke up he reached out for a bunch of grapes. But the vine had not got many bunches left because the fox had been so greedy. There was one beautiful big bunch hanging high up in the branches of the vine. He told the vine to give him those grapes. He forgot that she could not move as he could. Then he got angry again and threw sticks and stones at the bunch of grapes. The grapes began to smash as the stones hit them, until the bunch was just a mushy mess. But still they did not fall to the ground.

Then the fox got very angry indeed and went off into the forest on his own, to find a new vine to play tricks for. 'I'll show that vine that I don't need her any more', he thought to himself.

When the fox left, all the birds and the squirrels came back to the vine and she started to laugh again. The wind dropped by and told her more stories. The squirrels brought their babies and showed them how to make the vine giggle as they tickled her with their sharp little claws. And the scars of his name healed over until there was hardly a trace.

The fox wandered far and near but all he could find were vines with ordinary purple and green grapes. Nowhere could he find a vine with beautiful blue grapes that were so big and so sweet as his vine.

He wandered for many days until he suddenly realised how much he missed his vine. He went back through the forest and found her still growing beautiful and strong. He looked for the mark of his name but it was not there. She had grown new bark to cover over the marks he had made. When the fox saw that he became even angrier and started to cut the vine down. He hacked away at her branches and trunk and made more cuts than you could imagine, dear reader. The vine cried out and begged him to stop. 'I will grow lots of grapes for you if you play for me and make me laugh again.' She pleaded with the fox but he was too angry. He could not hear her words. The vine stopped saying anything and silently waited for him to stop cutting her.

The wind was wandering through the forest. He heard the cries of the vine and thought how sad she sounded. Then he heard her silence. He loved the vine. He blew hurriedly through the forest, bending all the trees as he went. 'Hurry, hurry,' all the trees called out to the wind as he passed them by.

When he saw what the fox was doing he called to the fox to stop cutting the vine down. The fox didn't listen to him either. Then the wind sucked in his cheeks as far as they could go and started to blow. He blew as hard as he could. The fox tried to carry on cutting the vine down but the wind was too strong for him. It blew him over and sent him tumbling over and over across the ground. Then the wind lifted the fox right up into the air and carried him far away, to another forest where there were no more vines. He told the fox never to come back to that forest again.

The fox was very sad to begin with. Then he told himself and his new friends in the new forest that the blue grapes had never been that special and that he would find something just as sweet to eat in this forest. And he played and made everyone laugh and they thought that it must be true, that the blue grapes were never that good anyway. He was such a jolly good fox.

The vine grew strong again. All the trees around her helped. Very soon she was as big and beautiful as ever. Sometimes she felt very sad and missed the fox playing under her branches but then she would remember how he had chased away her friends, and had carved her bark till the sap dripped, and smashed her grapes with stones. And worst of all she remembered how he had tried to cut her down. Then she was glad that he had gone. Now she could play with the squirrels and the birds whenever she wanted. She could grow her big beautiful blue grapes and give them to all her friends. She would live happily ever after.

# Thinking about 'The Fox and the Blue Grapes'

## IDENTIFYING THE THEMES

This story has many interpretations so, as before, see how many you can think of.
My list includes:

- domestic violence
- bullying
- jealousy
- fear and anger
- falling out with best friends
- cognitive dissonance and self deception
- understanding love
- listening and not listening
- trusting and not trusting.

### Domestic violence

This is a theme which is very difficult to discuss and yet is a common experience for many children. This story does not pass judgement on the characters but it does illustrate some of the complexities of the issue: for instance, the connection between love and fear, and how they can overlap in ways that become destructive if our inner voices are based on fear interpretations of life. The fox does not have a very strong intrinsic sense of self and is dependent on others to feel good and valued. He has learned how to make people laugh and be delighted with him, but he is too needy to be able to cope with any competition and his insecurity kicks in with a fear of loss. He cannot accept that the vine is able to love many (people) without detracting from her love for him. He is so busy extracting the love he needs that he forgets to return her love in positive ways that recognise her inner self. The hurt this inflicts on her makes her withdraw slightly, as a self protection mechanism. This makes him feel even more insecure and the vicious cycle continues with the fox feeling more and more threatened, expressed through anger which eventually gets out of control. In the end he destroys the very love which he so desperately wanted to keep, and like Aesop's fox, decides that the blue grapes weren't that good after all. He is sent away by the wind, representing whatever force does end such relationships, eg the law, extended family and friends, therapists etc. A child who is faced with violence can be helped to understand what is happening and not feel that they are somehow to blame. They need to recognise that the motivation for violence and aggression is always fear, therefore the perpetrator is the biggest victim and can be forgiven. They will lose more in the long run. By releasing the guilt and fear attached to violence, it is possible to grow from the experience, through forgiveness.

## Bullying

Very similar to domestic violence but usually occurs outside the family. Very often the victim of bullying doesn't understand why they are being picked on, but at an unconscious level they are fearful characters who do not have strong internal boundaries, and who in their own way give out messages that they are easy targets. The vine is unable to move and this represents her vulnerability. She is passive and allows others to come and take from her in return for very little except the feeling of being needed. The fox takes this to an extreme which nearly destroys her and she learns to be more careful with her generosity, restricting it to those she can trust.

## Jealousy

The fox is full of fear of losing his control and influence over the vine and is obsessed with keeping all her qualities, as expressed by the blue grapes, for himself. This is common in relationships where one partner has low self esteem and is using the other as a scaffold or prop. He is so jealous of her affection for others that he would do anything to keep them away and have all the blue grapes for himself, even if that means making the vine unhappy and actually less able to produce so many grapes. By restricting her, the fox is destroying the very qualities which he is so desperate to have. This often happens in relationships where one or both partners are too insecure and low in self esteem that they are dependent on others, yet destroy the other in their desperate sense of need, thereby making themselves feel superior but also triggering fear as their support system withdraws and disintegrates.

## Fear and anger
Fear is the basis of destruction of what could have been a very mutually fulfilling and rewarding relationship between the fox and the vine. Fear is the opposite of love and the source of all negative experiences. Anger is one of the most common manifestations of fear, a response which easily builds on itself until it becomes out of control. Anger is an attempt to control the source of fear but it usually has the opposite effect, of destroying love and trust. Thus the fox becomes more fearful as he becomes more angry. He is unable to control the vine because she has feelings which he is failing to recognise in his desperation. He is trying to manipulate her for his own needs, but she is an individual and therefore has her own needs, responses and understanding, which he cannot control. It is important to recognise this with everyone we come into contact with – both in relationships at home and at work.

## Falling out with best friends
For a child this can feel like the worst thing to happen, especially if their home life is secure and stable. Separation and loss are something that we must all experience in order to understand that love is the absence of fear. The fox and vine could be seen to be best friends who ended up in a very jealous and possessive situation which the child had difficulty coping with, or where the child is themselves the jealous friend who needs to see what they are doing in a detached way, so that they can think about the possible outcome of their behaviour.

## Cognitive dissonance and self deception
These are more or less the same thing and occur when we tell ourselves and others something which we know is not true but we will find as an excuse to justify until we eventually believe the new story. The dissonance is the sense of conflict that we feel about the known lie and we change our belief system in order to make the lie more comfortable, ie no longer a lie but the truth. The fox expresses his cognitive dissonance when he rejects the grapes and says they were not as sweet as he thought they were to begin with. He lies because he cannot bear the truth, which is that he was rejected by the vine and that he tried to destroy her. It is his own inability to recognise and face his own fear which becomes a destructive force in his life and gives him ever more reasons to feel fear and withdraw from life. The vine understands that he has made his own life worse that hers, because she has just gone back to the life she had before

he came along and, although she may miss the fun a little from time to time, she is glad to have escaped from his control games.

## Understanding love
The vine understands that love is giving and not expecting something in return; it is also living without fear, and she is generous in this part of her life to all who come near to her. The fox does not and is not able to love the vine or anyone else because he is too emotionally dependent on approval. He has a low self esteem that means he does not love himself. In many ways he is like Keith in the case studies. This story clearly shows that the vine loved the fox and would have continued to do so if he had valued her and respected the life she had before he came along. This is what he had been attracted to and what he became insanely jealous of, to the point of destruction.

The story also shows the vine as non vindictive and forgiving, a sign of how much love she has and how little fear there is in her life. Fear can attack love but a love without fear cannot be destroyed because it is the stronger emotion in the end. She trusts the wind and the other small creatures who come to play with her and this heals all the wounds that the fox has inflicted.

## Listening and not listening
The fox listens to what the vine says and to the others who come to visit her, but he hears them in a distorted way because of his own insecurity and fear. He hears them as threats, as beings who will come between him and his need fulfilment from the vine. To the fox his interpretation is the only real one because it is based on his perceptual bias of fear. We don't know the childhood experiences of the fox, we just see the result of the damage in his life and how his fear-based perceptual bias prevents him ever finding contentment or success in his life. He just runs from one disaster to another and never takes responsibility for his actions. This is why it is so important to love yourself in a simple acceptance and forgiving way that allows you to take responsibility and live without fear in your life.

## Trusting and not trusting
The fox is unable to trust anything or anyone in his life because he cannot trust himself. He has very weak boundaries and they are easily wiped out by the power of his fear. He behaves in ways which he finds repellent, but experiences such distress with himself that he convinces himself that the vine deserved it and was a fake, less good

than she was supposed to be. By contrast the vine trusts the fox and gives him her fruit which represents her love for him. She is shocked by the changes in him and sad for his fear but she cannot reach him because he listens with the perceptions of fear only. Nothing can get past that because he protects himself with massive barriers based on that fear, which allow little through except his expectations, which he fulfils for himself regardless of the efforts of the vine.

Whose loss is the greater? The lack of trust that the vine would always give him as many grapes he could eat, if he only let her live and continue all the parts of her life, shows how important it is for parents to teach their children to trust and for parents to be trustworthy for their children with honesty and openness. Megan in the end will learn that she cannot trust Keith and will start to keep parts of her life from him. He will fulfil his own fear there too because he cannot believe that anyone can be trusted – he cannot trust himself. The fox cannot trust anyone else until he has learned to trust himself and this is the key to trust. This aspect relates also to Violet in the next story: she held on to the trust in her instincts thanks to Old Mags and in spite of her parents. She did not lose sight of the power of love and belief in the inner self because she had learned to trust, so had the vine. The wind represents a position of authority, the law, a friend etc and his influence on the situation restores her trust in herself very quickly. One mistake does not destroy your self confidence but it will teach you valuable lessons.

# The Legend of Wildwood

'Violet, Violet, can you hear me?' The voice was so sweet, so gentle. It sang like the wind playing through hollow wood. Violet sighed but did not wake. 'Trouble is coming to the forest Violet. Trouble, and you must save us all.' Still Violet did not wake. 'We will tell you when it is time. Don't forget Violet, don't forget.' The singing stopped.

Violet woke up, rubbed her eyes and looked around. She was sure that someone had been talking to her but she was alone, as usual, in the forest. The sun was getting low. There were all sorts of stories about the spirits of the trees that lived there. Most people said it was all nonsense but they did not go into the forest at night either. Violet hurried home. 'Why are you so late?' her mother demanded as she hurried in through the door. 'I fell asleep by the tree with the twisted trunk. I came home as soon as I woke up. I was dreaming.'

Her mother looked worried. 'What dreams did you have?'

'I dreamed that someone was talking to me, asking me to save the forest.'

Violet's mother got cross at that and told her not to go back into the forest ever again, especially not back to the tree with the twisted trunk. But whenever Violet asked her mother why, she would not say any more and got more and more cross.

That night her father came home looking especially pleased. He hugged Violet as he came through the door.

'We're going to be rich Violet, we're going to be rich. We're going to have all the lovely things that other people have instead of scraping a living from the fields and forest.' And he danced around the tiny living room, bumping into the table and chairs, knocking over the candlesticks.

Violet looked at her father with disbelief. He was never this happy. He usually came home ready to be cross with her because of something she had done or not done.

Her mother called out from the kitchen at the back of the

house.

'Tell me what has been decided, then.'

'We're going to sell the forest. The lumber company will pay us and do all the work and then tell us how to start all over again. It was agreed at the village council meeting.'

Violet's mother came out of the kitchen, rubbing the flour off her hands with a cloth. 'Does that mean I won't have to work in the fields and in the kitchen all day?'

'Yes my love, we'll be able to have whatever we want. The lumber company are going to set up a shop in the village and we can buy things from them.'

'What's a shop and what's buy?' asked Violet.

'Buying is when you give someone money and in return they give you something you want. You can use money to buy different things. A shop is a place which has lots of things to buy.'

Violet puzzled over this a little longer.

'Then why do we need this? The village council makes sure that everything is shared out fairly and that everyone is fed and sheltered for the year. Then we have all the festivals for each part of the year and the gifts from the forest?' Her father held up his hand but Violet carried on, 'And why do they want to buy the forest? They can't take it away.'

'Oh why are you asking so many questions?' he said crossly. 'They will cut the trees down and take them away. What do you think?'

Violet burst into tears and screamed, 'No! No! They can't, they mustn't.'

Her father was angry now. 'Go to your room,' he ordered, 'and don't come down until you stop these silly ideas about the forest being your friend. It's just a bunch of silly old trees.'

Violet could not understand why her father and mother did not love the forest as she did. She lay on her bed, buried her face in the covers and cried herself to sleep. As she slept she dreamed that the forest was calling to her.

'Go to Old Mags. She will tell you what to do,' the voice sang, flying on the wind and through the window into Violet's dreams.

The following morning Violet woke and knew what she must do. She climbed out of bed and left the cottage before her mother and father were up. It was still dark as she crept through the village and out to the little hut at the edge of the forest where Old Mags lived. No one really spoke to Old Mags, but they all sent for her when they were ill. She knew the wisdom of the plants in the forest and she could deliver a child without any pain for the mother. Everyone in the village was a bit scared of her but could not admit it. Violet trembled and shivered as she went. 'It's the cold,' she told herself, reluctant to admit that it was really the thought of going to see Old Mags on her own.

Old Mags was waiting for Violet and opened the door for her. She listened while Violet told her what had happened.

'Shall we take some lemonade out into the garden and watch the sun rise? Then I'll tell you a story about the forest when it was very young.' They sat down on a rickety old bench in the corner of Mag's garden and watched the sky turn pink and yellow, getting brighter and brighter. 'I watch the sun rise everyday. Then I know that it is a new day, a new birth and new things will happen.' They sat in silence until the sun had risen higher than the trees. Then, sitting in the sunshine, Violet listened while Mags told her the legend of Wildwood.

---

Once upon a time, long ago when stories were just beginning, there lived a young man called Woodwind. His mother named him after the gentle calling sounds he made whenever he heard the wind blowing from his cradle, which sounded like the wind blowing through the trees. He loved the land and liked to go walking far off, to see what he could see and hear what he could hear. He feared nothing and was always happy. He knew that the shadows only made the light seem brighter.

One day he walked for a long time, to a forest in a very distant land. As he walked he heard a beautiful sound coming from deep in the trees. The sounds called to him. They spoke of love and sadness, beauty and death. They spoke of time, the seasons, and a wisdom that goes beyond all of this. He kept following the sounds until he came to a small group of trees deep in the heart of the forest. There sat a beautiful young woman, singing and dancing among the trees, her long green and gold hair swirling and twirling around her as she danced.

Woodwind stayed behind the trees and listened. He watched her for a long time, until the shadows joined hands and danced with her, until the light was almost gone. Then she stood still, lifted her arms up to the night sky and slipped away into the trees at the other side of the clearing. Woodwind tried to follow her but as he reached the centre of the clearing she disappeared. He looked everywhere and felt saddened by her disappearance. Finally, realising how dark the night had become and that he no longer knew which direction he had come from, Woodwind lay down in the centre of the clearing and went to sleep. As he slept he dreamed that all the trees around the edge of the clearing had come to life and were standing over him. At first they were very angry with him and shook their fists to drive him away. Then the young woman returned and waved her arms around in a circle above her head. And the others started to dance round him, slowly and softly so as not to wake him. All night they circled him until the first light of dawn came creeping over the tops of the trees. Then they all quietly became trees again.

When Woodwind woke, he rubbed his eyes and looked around. Just the circle of trees. The sun rose in the sky and started to warm him. He wondered if the dreams had been real. Just then, the young woman slipped out from behind a tree.

'Why are you here? It is not allowed for humans to come to the place of the dancing trees.'

'I have never heard of such a place. I was walking and I heard your singing. I had to follow. It called me. But when you stopped singing, I could not find you. I could not see where you had gone.'

'Humans cannot hear the songs of the Dryads, they only hear the rustling of our leaves or the creaking of our branches.'

'Your song is the most beautiful song that I have ever heard. I want to listen to it for the rest of my life. Will you sing for me again?'

The woman made a deep rich sound of hollow wood being drummed. Woodwind realised that she was laughing and he laughed with her.

'What is your name young man?'

'I am called Woodwind after the noises I made when I was young.'

'With a name like that you must be able to hear the songs of the Dryads. You are welcome. It is many years since men and Dryads were able to work together and hear each other's words. My name is Silvrine and this is my tree. I carry all the seasons of the tree in me.'

She pointed to a tall graceful silver birch tree, with beautiful silver bark and light fluttering leaves that hung down from its branches. Then Woodwind could see that her hair drifted as the leaves moved and fluttered in the gentle breeze, green for the spring and golden for the autumn.

Silvrine and Woodwind sat and talked for many days. Each night she would leave him, for a Dryad will die if they leave their tree for too long. Woodwind slept each night in the circle of trees, guarded by all the Dryads. As the days went by Silvrine told of the history of men and Dryads. Of how her great great grandfather had followed the men into battle, had fought on the side of the Druids, the men of Oak, and many had lost their lives. But the men made too many battles and the Dryads lost too many of their kind. Once the Dryad has died, the tree will become a tree with no spirit and will die, a long slow death.

As Woodwind and Silvrine talked, they grew to love each other.

'If I leave my tree and live with you and have a family, our children will be of the forest and I will die the death of a human. My tree will die when I do.'

'You must never leave your tree for me.'

Woodwind and Silvrine talked for many more months and the days became cold. The Dryads covered Woodwind with their fallen leaves and threw down branches for shelter. They gave him nuts to eat and cared for him as one of their own. But Silvrine and Woodwind became more and more sad each evening as she had to leave him.

Eventually they went to the elders, the Dryads of the Great Oaks that stood sentinel over the whole forest. Oakhorn, the oldest, wisest Dryad in the forest, knew their story. His wise old heart went out to them. He remembered the love between men and Dryads from long ago. He listened, then sent them away so he could think. Oakhorn knew the special times when a Dryad could leave their tree. But only for love.

Oakhorn watched them both over the next few days. He saw the love that Woodwind and Silvrine shared but his heart was heavy, for the children of men and Dryads must live in and love the forest if they are to continue. Silvrine would die as a human sooner than Woodwind, but that she could return to her tree at the end and never leave it again. There she could live as the tree for the full life of a Dryad, which is many hundreds of years.

Oakhorn thought very hard about their future and what it might mean to the forest. The Dryads had chosen to keep away from humans because they did not understand their love of fighting and death. Dryads love the seasons and the creatures that live in their boughs. Eventually he decided to tell them what he knew. He called to them.

'Silvrine, it is true that Dryads may not leave their tree for long. What is also true from long ago is that they may if it is for love. But you must return to your tree for one month every year and you may only leave for twenty years. After that you must never leave it again. Your tree will not die if you return. You can choose what you wish to do.'

Silvrine and Woodwind looked at each other and the love in their hearts spoke for them.

'I will do this. It is a short time but better than nothing.' Silvrine held out her hand to Woodwind and they danced a little together around Oakhorn's mighty presence.

Silvrine nodded, 'there will be many children who can keep Woodwind as he grows old.'

Oakhorn shook his head slowly. 'You may have one child. This child will have many more children. They will care for both of you.'

Silvrine and Woodwind had a son whom they called Wildwood. Each winter, Silvrine returned to her tree for one month. Wildwood grew up in the forest and everything was provided for him. The Dryads would dance with him in the evenings, and teach him of their gifts. The chestnuts and cobnuts gave him food, the mighty oaks gave him wood to make shelters, the willows that grew along the banks of the river gave him boughs to make baskets. When he became a young man, Silvrine took him to one side and told him what must happen.

'My son, my time has passed and soon I must leave. I must return to my tree. You have grown into a man and I will always be with you in the forest. But now you must find a love of your own and bring her here to live. Your father will teach you how to grow food for your children. The forest will always provide for you and your children and their children but you must teach them all about the Dryads and never let them cut the trees. You must celebrate with the forest for each harvest it gives. When you need wood, the trees will give you their branches with the wind. Never never cut the living trees for you will be cutting your brothers and sisters of the forest. You will have children and a happy life if you choose carefully. Go my son, the birds of the forest will bring me word of you on your adventure,' and she kissed Wildwood for the last time as his mother.

Wildwood shed many tears as he walked through the forest. Where they fell a small plant grew, with pale mauve flowers. The trees showed him the way back to the land of humans as he walked through them, touching each one as he passed in greeting. As he passed Oakhorn, he heard the huge old oak sigh. He held his hand against the bark for a long time. He felt the love and wisdom of his friend and guardian of the forest. Then he knew that he must go and do as his mother told him.

A few weeks later, the birds brought the message that he had reached a village and met a young woman. Her family had taken him in and taught him the ways of men. Silvrine sighed a long sigh.

Her twenty years was ended and she must leave Woodwind in human form forever. They stood with their arms entwined around each other for a long time. Gradually their feet became roots and their arms became branches that danced and swayed with the wind. And gradually they both became one with Silvrine's tree. It was something that had never happened before, a human taking the form of a Dryad and even Oakhorn watched in wonder at the power of love to transform those who truly love each other.

Wildwood returned to the forest with Bryony, his bride. They walked through the forest and all the Dryads welcomed Bryony. Eventually they came to the clearing and saw the tree all twisted and twined around itself. Then Wildwood knew and sat at the foot of the tree and told his parents of his love. He heard the rustle of their leaves and the haunting sounds of their great hearts echoing throughout the whole forest, and he knew that they were together.

He made garlands from the violets that grew around the clearing and hung them around the great tree that was his parents. Each year, at the same time, he made the garland of violets and gave thanks to his parents for their protection. And for each gift that the forest gave to Wildwood and Bryony, they thanked the forest with dances and songs that Silvrine had taught him. Wildwood and Bryony had many children and lived well within the forest. They were careful to teach their children all that Silvrine had told Wildwood, so that the trees were never felled.

The children grew and had more families, until a whole village grew up living in the forest. For many hundreds of years the stories were passed down from parent to child, that the forest would continue to provide all that they needed as long as they only took what they did need and no more, so that there was enough to go round for everyone, including all the animals, birds and insects that lived in the woods and round the fields. They called the village Wildwood, after their father who had taught them to love the forest and live in peace with all the animals. Everyone knew that as long as the trees were never cut, they would have all that they needed and could live happily.

---

Violet sighed. She felt warm in the sunshine. 'That's a lovely story, Mags. Is it true?'

'Does it feel true?' said Mags. Violet nodded. 'Then believe what you feel inside. Now then, what does this story tell you about your father's news and your dreams at the roots of the old tree?'

Violet thought for a little while and suddenly it all made sense.

'That tree is Silvrine and Woodwind's tree, it was Silvrine calling to me but she can never leave her tree, she can only call to me. She knows what is to happen to the forest and she wants me to help. But how can I stop them? What can I do to stop my father and all the rest of the men in the village from cutting down the trees?' Violet started to cry at the thought of so much responsibility.

'Trust your instincts and you will know what to do,' said old Mags. 'Go into the forest now and it will show you. Just open your eyes and see whatever you can see.'

Violet thought for a while. She knew that Old Mags was right. She ran to the council and cried out that they must not forget the stories of the forest. Surely everyone saw that the forest gave them all they needed, the stories must be true. And what would happen to the festivals?

'Be quiet, Violet, everyone knows you are mad,' they said to her, 'go away and keep your old fashioned ideas to yourself.'

Violet ran from one family to the next, crying out that they were wrong, that the trees would die and they would be left with nothing. They all turned away from her, pushing her with their hands and their hard hearts and stares.

Eventually, exhausted, Violet returned home and lay down on her bed and cried. No one listened to Violet. Instead the people in the village started to argue about who owned the trees and the land, who would be in charge of the cutting and selling and who would be responsible for replanting and taking care of the new trees. The council argued for many days and nights. Violet's father put himself in charge of the organising and became the most experienced and knowledgeable about trade practices. He negotiated the deals with the lumber company and the trees were sold.

The noise of the machines cutting the trees was matched by the noise of the great trees hitting the ground and crushing the smaller ones in their path. Each day more trees were cut, and their songs at night became more and more sad. There was noise and dust everywhere.

Violet walked through the forest each night, just ahead of the great cutting machines, and touched each tree in turn and said goodbye. The trees shook their branches sadly and gave her a little seed from each of their kind. Their sad songs whispered to her, 'save us, grow our seeds so that we can live again'. And Violet made a little garden in the corner of her land and planted the seeds the great forest gave her, and wept for the sadness of their songs each night. She stopped playing with any of the other children in the village. They just called her crazy Violet and laughed at her even more than before.

When the great cutting machines reached the two trees that were twisted into one, a mighty crash was heard and the whole tree split into two halves, then crumbled into dust, right before the eyes of the men driving the machine. They could not believe their eyes and told the villagers that evening at a council meeting.

'See, I told you that the trees had hearts,' said Violet. 'That is the tree of Silvrine and Woodwind.'

But the woodsmen laughed and said that it was just a very old tree that was probably half dead already, eaten away from the inside by insects. It was probably dangerous and would have been blown over in the next big wind.

Each day the sky was full of more birds who had lost their homes. The rabbits and squirrels came into the fields and started to eat the food the villagers grew because there was no food in the forest. The people in the village asked the council what they should do to stop the rabbits eating all their vegetables. Some people argued that they should stop cutting down the forest and let it all grow back. Some villagers argued that they should just stop the rabbits eating the food. 'How will we do that?' cried everyone at the meeting, 'the rabbits are starving too'. They had to start killing the rabbits because they were eating the vegetables so fast there would be none left for the winter. Violets father put his hand up when everyone said that they couldn't possibly do this. 'We have no choice,' he said, 'we will starve if we do not kill them. Besides the woodsmen said that rabbit stew is very tasty.'

The children of the village suddenly found that when they went into the fields to play, all the rabbits ran away from them, so did the squirrels and the voles, the frogs and the toads and the mice. The children cried that they had nothing to play with any more. The council arranged to buy pretend animals. These animals were soft and warm, but they did not move. It cost three whole trees to pay for the new toys.

There were no more festivals, and the families in the village did not talk to each other as they had. Instead they looked to see who had got a new chair or curtains. The houses started to have fences put up around them and new gates on their fences. Some families were making their houses bigger, they were taking parts of the fields and common land to make bigger and bigger houses. They began to put up bigger and bigger fences, and bigger and bigger gates on their fences. And as the fences got higher and higher and the houses got bigger and bigger, the people laughed less and less. Nearly all the trees in the forest were cut down. Each tree brought less and less into the village and the villagers were worrying how they would heat their homes this winter, how they would feed their animals from the nuts and how they would bring the forest into their homes that winter.

Eventually the villagers went to see the village council and demanded to know what the woodsmen would do for them when the trees ran out. How would they feed their families and heat their homes and live their lives? And what about all the festivals? There was nothing to celebrate now. They needed their forest back. When were the woodsmen going to plant the new trees and give them enough food? Violet's father wrung his hands and agreed to go and ask the woodsmen. They just laughed.

'We gave you the rewards for your forest, as you all agreed. It is up to you to sort out your own problems. We are busy and have new trees to cut.'

And the woodsmen would not give them the answers when they asked for them. The woodsmen just said, 'cut down the last trees and we will give you what you agreed.' So the villagers sadly watched the woodsmen cut down the last few trees, until there were no more standing at all and the whole forest was silent and dead.

Violet went to see the village council but found them in tears. The woodsmen had gone away and no one knew where they had gone. They had taken all their beautiful forest and left them with nothing. No one knew what to do. The council meeting was silent with the sadness of the whole village. Then Violet, very quietly, said 'Come and look next to my house'.

'It's just mad Violet again, what can she possibly know?' said the council.

'If you come and look, you will know. At least it is better than sitting here.' The villagers heard her words and saw a wisdom they had not seen before.

'What can you have, Violet?'

'I have the forest. I saved the forest while you were busy helping to cut it down.'

Violet led them to a small patch of ground near to the fence that had been put around her house. She pointed with her finger, and there the villagers saw a little oak tree growing, and next to it a little chestnut tree, and a holly, and a yew, nut trees and beech trees. Willows. Ash trees. Silver birch trees, and more and more tiny baby trees. Then they realised that the little girl who they had all laughed at had young trees growing from all the old trees in the forest.

Her tiny trees were carefully taken to where the old forest had once grown so proud and strong and the villagers made a festival to celebrate the planting of the new trees. The fences were taken down and used to keep the families warm in the winter and the land was shared with the animals again. The rabbits and squirrels used the soft warm fabric of the toy animals to make the nests for their babies until the trees were big enough. The people in the village started to smile and talk to each other again. They stopped looking to see what each family had got and started to share everything again.

The village council made Violet the new leader and asked her to forgive them for their laughter. She did immediately, for she knew that they would listen to her now. No one would ever say that there was no such thing as a Dryad again.

It took many years for the forest to grow back and many old people said that it was never the same again. The festival of the new planting became the most important festival of the village every year after that, and no one ever was allowed to forget the lesson they had learned.

# Thinking about the Legend of Wildwood

## IDENTIFYING THE THEMES

What are your first thoughts and impressions of this story? It has many layers and includes a story within the story. It contains values, cautions, wisdom and myths. Does your list include any of the following:

- the importance of listening to older and younger people in society
- the importance of remembering old wisdom and teaching
- the importance of staying true to your heart and not following the majority
- the importance of parents listening to their children
- the abuse of power?

What areas of life could it be applied to:

- taking drugs or breaking other social rules
- fighting for what you believe in the face of criticism
- recognising the destructive nature of fear, pride and envy
- respecting all members of the family whatever their age
- learning to listen and communicate with open minds
- positive self image for girls and womanhood
- respecting the environment
- learning to live without the newest designer labels
- the importance of contentment
- the destructiveness of greed and arrogance?

### Listening to people of all ages

One of the clearest themes in this story is that the only two people who do not follow the lead from the council are an old woman and a young girl. In our society these represent two of the most disempowered sections of the population and yet it is evident from this story that they have the clearest overview of the whole situation. Often it is the simplicity of childhood which can see straight to the centre of an issue and not become clouded with secondary considerations. Similarly older people have been through enough ups and downs to see what really matters.

In this story Old Mags is rather like the old wisewoman matriarchal figure in so many stories. She represents the wisdom of old age but also the third age of womanhood: the hag. Our culture sees this stage of life as ugly and is afraid of it. The image of an old woman is not generally seen as positive unless it is in terms of how young and glamorous they are for their age. This story allows a contemplation of superficial values of women and is especially powerful in this respect because both men and women need to embrace the beauty of wise woman images.

The three women in this story represent the three stages of female development: the young girl who is learning to trust her instincts, the adult woman engaged in daily life and family considerations, and the old woman who has time to forget herself and exist in peace with her surroundings, knowing that she has lived each stage of her life fully meeting her potential. Old Mags is unaffected by the fear from the other villagers, she sees it for what it is and she is content to live her life and offer what she can to those who ask. She has found contentment and is in touch with her true self.

Violet is still trying to establish her individuality. She is very intuitive and a little bit unusual in this. Her parents see her as 'just a child' and assume that her dreams are nothing. She is being denied her true self. The story shows how hard it is for a child who is not fully listened to, who is ridiculed for being in tune with herself in a way that is misunderstood by those too busily engaged in a material life to notice beyond that. Her mother and father have lost touch with the part of themselves that experiences the beauty of natural living things and the joy of existence, they have become caught up in their practical life and have become very negative as a result.

Violet has a recognition of all things beautiful in her and she feels it very strongly, but she is beginning to be affected by her parents' attitudes and those of the other villagers. She is beginning to feel fear of the forest at night and of Old Mags. It is her own dreams which tell her to trust the two things she is being told she should not trust. Through this she reaches her own intuitive self again and quietly goes about her life and fulfils her role. Then she waits until someone will listen and recognise herself. This is the turning inward which many people experience when they find that contact with themselves and can finally show their true selves and live without fear. But until the people in the village are ready to hear she remains silent and quietly fulfils her purpose.

### The importance of remembering old teaching
There was a legend which went back to the beginning of the history of the village and its founding parents. It followed a very clear message of living in harmony with the forest and never cutting down the trees. They would give all that was needed. This is a theme that is prevalent throughout all major philosophies, belief systems and religions. The story demonstrates how important it is to be content with what you have and not want more. The majority of the village rejected the legend as old rubbish, just a story and nothing more. They closed their minds to its central wisdom because it no longer seemed relevant to their modern lives. Progress must clear away all out of date attitudes. And so they listened to the new philosophies of materialism and the village lost its harmony. The wisdom within the old myth still held true in the present because it had a simple truth at heart: live in harmony with yourself and your environment and all you need will be provided.

The destruction of the forest symbolises the destruction felt by so many people whose lives have taken them away from the centre of contentment. Many young people are desperate to have the latest designer label and parents struggle to find the money to provide it. The need to have things to make you feel good has subsumed the knowledge and teaching which tell us to be content with what we have; to believe in yourself and what you inner truth tells you. Most people are so detached from their inner selves that they do not even believe there is this inner truth, yet those who take time to look inward will find it and the peace which goes with it. It is not necessary to be religious to experience this inner peace and contentment.

### The importance of staying true to yourself and not following the majority
Violet and Old Mags did not get caught up in the enthusiasm of the village for these new promises. Inside each of them there was the higher truth which made them circumspect and singled them both

out for ridicule in different ways. Yet by sticking to their higher truths they were able to put things right. For some children who have this sense of themselves and who are not listened to, it can be very lonely to live with this sense of isolation and yet they become unhappy if they try to conform. The pressure on everyone to conform is enormous and this story can help us to see that we should never give in because the truth will come through in the end. Both Violet and Mags are able to go above their fear and to stay close to their inner truths. They have a firm set of beliefs and value in themselves which does not allow them to be swayed by anyone else. This is one of the most important assets for a successful life and yet it can seem pointless to fight against the majority. Many people will tell you that you are making life harder for yourself and you should just keep quiet and go along with things for an easy life. Life is not hard unless you fight it, but although confirmity might make life seem easier at the outset it will become harder in the end.

The people in the village went along with what seems like a good idea at the time, something to make life easier, and Violet has a really hard time of it. But in the end the whole village is faced by a much harder and potentially devastating problem which only Violet can put right. She had to stay quiet and carry out her work in silence, with the burden of ridicule upon her, but she was triumphant. The easy way is rarely the way to success in a whole sense. It may be a way of life which brings a veneer of success but more is possible.

### The importance of listening to children

Children who are not listened to are being denied their own truths. For adults, however simple or naive it may seem, whatever a child believes should be treated with respect. We are too quick in society to reject anything which might be demanding or challenging to our desire to live without responsibility, but in the end it will come back to us. Children mirror back to us that which we need to look at in ourselves. Violet mirrored back to her parents their dissatisfaction and greed and they did not like it, so became angry with her. They rejected the message she tried to show them, they dismissed her and became unavailable to her. She turned to someone else for her inner guidance and development. To someone who did listen.

### The abuse of power

This is a story of people who were given self government and who forgot the important rules that went with it. They were given a shared power based on equality and respect for all that they had, including each other. With all power, even self government, comes responsibility for decisions and outcomes. Most of the people in the village had lived such a comfortable life that they had forgotten how to take decisions and had abdicated their responsibility to an outside influence.

In many ways we do this through relationships. We make someone else responsible for our well-being and blame them when things go wrong. If a parent loses control and then blames the child for doing something to make them angry, they are abdicating responsibility for their own behaviour. If a child makes a mistake and is not helped to take responsibility for their actions in a loving, learning way they will be unable to take responsibility for their own welfare and will always blame someone else for their mistakes. Only Violet and Old Mags remain responsible for their own actions in the face of much obstruction and difficulty, thereby staying true to themselves and rescuing the others from their own misfortune, but in a way that obliges them to recognise and take responsibility for their mistakes. They allow Violet to guide them back to the intuitions which kept the truth alive.

# Glossary

**Amygdala**. Part of the limbic system; there are two, one found on each side of the brain. They specifically relate to emotional responses and emotional memory. Research into life without the amygdala shows people to be uninterested in other people and unmoved by emotional experiences. It responds to expressions of emotion, eg tears and cuddles. It can work before the thinking brain, the neocortex, has even had a chance to respond. According to Daniel Goleman it is the key to emotional intelligence from a physiological perspective. It has direct access to information from the senses and can trigger the fear reactions of fight or flight rather like a smoke alarm, before the conscious brain has noticed anything in particular.

**Barriers**. These are protection shields which prevent us being open to others and are based on fear. They are rigid and cause emotional blockages.

**Boundaries**. This is a filtering system where we can recognise what is important and what is potentially harmful to us. They are flexible and allow emotional development and growth.

**Fight or flight**. This is the automatic response to danger. Physically it produces the following changes: heart rate, breathing rate and blood pressure increased, secretion of saliva suppressed, pupils dilated, blood vessels in limbs dilated, digestion slowed down, skin becomes less sensitive to pain, bladder muscles relax, adrenal glands excrete extra adrenaline and noradrenaline, liver releases extra energy stored as glucose, emotion experienced very intensely.

It can be triggered by either the amygdala or the neocortex. It activates the body into an alert, ready for action, state, with all the body systems on a highly sensitive response to any trigger. Any sense of feeling threatened mostly produces a response of anger, which, combined with the alert condition of the body, is more likely to produce a fight, either emotional or physical, than a flight response.

**Limbic system.** The limbic system is a ring of brain structures which circle the lower brain on both sides. It is the old brain and developed responses to emotional stimuli before the development of the neocortex or the thinking brain. It is linked both to the neocortex and to the automatic response mechanisms, which means that it is controlled not by the neocortex, but by the predominant emotional neural response to early life experience. Thus a childhood based on fear will lead to a very sensitive fear response for a far wider range of stimuli than a childhood based on love.

**Mirroring.** This is the effect of experiencing something in yourself through the eyes of another. The whole of our experience is feedback from the thoughts which created it. The world and all its aspects are mirrors of our own internal thought patterns, expectations and interpretations, beliefs and predictions, family scripts and agendas. Our experience of the outer world mirrors our inner world. It is a useful learning technique because it allows us to recognise things about ourselves that we are not consciously aware of, and thereby to make changes towards our own emotional growth and fulfilment. It allows us to accept our mistakes and forgive ourselves and to take responsibility for our own lives and life choices. A negative experience always offers an important lesson to be learned.

**Need.** Either a physical or a perceived requisite for survival. Physical needs are basic survival requisites such as food, shelter, sensory stimulation and comfort. Emotional needs vary from person to person according to how emotionally competent they are. An emotionally needy person is dependent on others to make them feel good because they are unable to fulfil their own needs. The emotionally competent individual has a stronger understanding of their own emotional responses and is intrinsically sustained and self sufficient.

**Reframe.** Looking at the same situation from a different perspective, such as a change in perception of childhood difficulties from being you as the victim to you as the person you are because of the experiences. Usually it is the transformation from a negative perception of events to a positive outcome.

# Further Reading

*The Chosen Child Syndrome*, Dr P Love and J Robinson (Piatkus Books).
*Emotional Intelligence*, Daniel Goleman (Bloomsbury Publishing Plc).
*Families and How to Survive Them*, Skynner and Cleese (Mandarin Paperbacks).
*The Heart of Parenting*, John Gottman and J Declaire (Bloomsbury Publishing Plc).
*How to Talk so Kids will Listen and Listen so Kids will Talk*, Faber and Mazlish (Avon Books, New York).
*Love is Letting go of Fear*, Gerald G Jampolsky MD (Celestial Books, California).
*That's Not What I Meant*, Derborah Tannen (Virago).
*When Parents Love Too Much*, Ashner and Meyerson (Random Century Ltd).
*Women Who Run With The Wolves*, Clarissa Pinkola Estes (Rider Books – Random House Group Ltd).
*You Just Don't Understand*, Deborah Tannen (Virago).

# Useful Addresses

**DEALING WITH BULLYING**

Kidscape, 152 Buckingham Palace Road, London SW1 9TR. Tel: (0171) 730 3300. Monday–Friday 10–4. For more information send an sae.

Childline. Tel: 0800 111 111. 24 hours a day.

Anti-Bullying Campaign. Tel: (0171) 378 1446. Monday–Friday 9.30–5.

Most local health clinics and doctors' surgeries have information about local youth counselling services or can put you in touch with family therapy teams and counsellors.

For details of one-day and weekend workshops for parenting skills and personal development, telephone Sylvia Clare on (0181) 778 8156 or e-mail her on sylvia.clare@btinternet.com

# Index

achievement, 14, 22, 43, 55
agenda, 32, 34, 38, 122
amyglada, 11, 12
anger, 13, 18, 32, 34, 66, 71
anxiety, 13
assumptions, 15, 27, 28, 58

balance, 44, 71
barriers, 55, 59–60, 73, 122
behaviour, 21, 33-4, 36, 62
blocks, 54, 58, 61
body language, 15
boundaries, 36, 59–60, 63, 65, 73, 104, 122

care, 35
case studies, 18, 19–22, 41, 50
cerebral cortex/neocortex, 12
challenge, 28, 34, 120
changes, 26, 34, 61
choices, 21, 24
communication, 15–19, 24, 35, 46
conflict, 14, 67
conformity, 73–4
confrontation, 72, 120
control, 20, 26, 32, 44, 52, 70, 103

development, 46
difficult,
  experiences, 44, 46, 49
  feelings, 18
  thoughts, 19, 103
discipline, 57, 62–3
double-bind, 21, 35
dreams, 79, 81, 118

emotions, 11–15, 21
empathy, 16-21, 27, 46, 52, 58, 65, 79
energy, 32, 39, 64
exercises, 14, 16, 58, 65
expectations, 15
external references, 20, 22, 74

fear, 11–13, 18–22, 48, 53–4, 59, 63, 71, 103–5, 118
feelings, 21, 68
forgiveness, 46, 67, 104

growth, 35, 46, 55
guidance, 120
guilt, 13, 22, 36, 48, 50, 53–4, 60, 71

humiliation, 58–9
hypocrisy, 62

imagination, 76–7
incidental learning, 77–9
inner child, 31, 47
intuition, 15, 46, 69, 118

# Index

joy, 11, 46
judgement, 51

knowledge, 46, 63, 73, 76

learning, 12, 26, 35, 79
  dimensions, 47
  tasks, 48–50
limbic system, 11, 123
listening, 17, 53, 62, 65, 78, 101, 117, 120
loneliness, 89–90

meta-message, 15, 21, 34, 54–5, 58, 59, 67, 75
mirroring, 26–7, 32–4, 38, 62, 66, 120, 123
mistakes, 35, 37, 44, 46, 51
myths, 81, 119

negative attitudes, 48, 72
  emotions, 64
  experiences, 30, 31, 32, 46, 60, 62

openness, 61, 68
opportunity, 24, 26, 28, 34, 35, 52, 53, 66

parenting, 27
  expectations, 43
  experiences, 30
  skills, 28, 32, 44
  styles, 28, 39, 43
patterns, 32, 34, 55
peace (inner), 40–41, 119

personal development, 41
positive attitudes, 30, 38, 70, 72
power, 15, 32–3, 36–8, 48, 53, 117, 120
problems, 25, 120

reframing, 80, 123
relationships, 18, 24, 40
resistance, 34, 61
response, 11, 27, 31, 72
revenge, 53
rules, 58, 62

self actualisation, 22–3, 34, 41–2, 53
self knowledge, 17, 36, 46, 74
shame, 60, 65, 68, 71
skills, 16, 31
society, 24, 33, 38, 61, 117
story-telling, 76–7, 81
success, 22, 24, 27, 48, 72–5, 120
support, 53, 56, 64, 70–73, 93

teaching, 26, 57, 66
thoughts, 17
trust, 26, 36, 46–48, 73, 101, 105, 119

unconscious, 65, 77, 80, 81
understanding, 16, 44, 101

value systems, 30
violence, 24, 25, 50, 52, 58, 76, 101–2

## Some other titles in this series

**HAVING A BABY**
**How to prepare for and manage pregnancy and the birth of your baby**

Dr Stavia Blunt

This book is a step-by-step guide taking you from the decision to have a baby, through to conception, pregnancy and delivery of the baby, and finally into the early post-natal period. The contents include: deciding to have a baby, discovering you are pregnant, monitoring your pregnancy, caring for yourself and your baby during pregnancy, managing problems in pregnancy, going into labour, discovering your baby, and returning to the non-pregnant state. Dr Stavia Blunt is a consultant physician and mother of two young children.

*160pp. illus. 1 85703 348 5.*


**PARENTING PRE-SCHOOL CHILDREN**
**How to cope with common behavioural problems**

Paul Stallard

Being a parent is undoubtedly the most responsible and demanding job people ever do – yet there is no training. Often when young children display challenging and demanding behaviour parents feel isolated and doubt their parenting abilities. This book reassures parents that such behaviour is common – a normal part of growing up. It provides parents and childcare professionals with clear ideas about how good behaviour can be encouraged, plus step-by-step guidance on how difficulties can be resolved. Paul Stallard is a Chartered Clinical Psychologist with two young children of his own. He works in the Health Service helping parents to find effective ways of dealing with their children's difficulties.

*144pp. illus. 1 85703 266 7.*